Small-wheeled pedal machines

– a better way of cycling

EARTHWORLD is a brand new imprint in the house of Veloce Publishing, showcasing innovative and thought-provoking books that are informative and entertaining. Produced to the same high quality of content and presentation as our existing books, EARTHWORLD is set to push the boundaries and expand horizons.

Also from Earthworld:

Discovering Engineering (Julian Edgar) – *Visit the sites of engineering feats that changed the world*

Mr Trump goes to Washington (Michael Mayor) – *Political satire in 3D graphic novel form*

Dairy Cows & Duck Races (Philip Dixon) – *Tales of a young farmer*

Coming soon ...

Peugeot Cycles (Brian Long) – *A celebration of the Peugeot brand during the golden years of cycling*

The Book of the Leica R-series Cameras (Brian Long) – *The definitive history of Leica's SLRs*

Mum's not the word – Childless, Childfree (Denise Felkin) – *A photographic essay challenging perceptions of women and motherhood*

www.veloce.co.uk

First published in June 2019 by Veloce Publishing Limited, Veloce House, Parkway Farm Business Park, Middle Farm Way, Poundbury, Dorchester DT1 3AR, England.
Tel +44 (0)1305 260068 / Fax 01305 250479 / e-mail info@veloce.co.uk / web www.veloce.co.uk or www.velocebooks.com.
ISBN: 978-1-787114-01-2 UPC: 6-36847-01401-8
Typesetting, design and page make-up all by Veloce Publishing Ltd on Apple Mac. Printed in India by Parksons Graphics.

Small-wheeled pedal machines

– a better way of cycling

Julian Edgar

EARTHWORLD
EXPANDING HORIZONS

Contents

Introduction 5

Chapter 1 Design 7

Chapter 2 Fixed-frame bikes 21

Chapter 3 Folding bikes 31

Chapter 4 Recumbent trikes.. 42

Chapter 5 Commuting 51

Chapter 6 Touring 57

Chapter 7 Restoration and rebuilding....................................... 75

Index.. 95

Introduction

Welcome to the world of small-wheeled pedal machines!

Whether you're commuting, touring or just riding for fun, bikes (and trikes) with small wheels have huge advantages. Those advantages are covered in more detail later, but in short, small-wheeled bikes are portable, nimble and can carry large loads. In many situations, that makes them much more practical than conventional large-wheeled bikes.

So how did I discover small-wheel pedal machines?

As with many people, I grew up riding a conventional bike. Then as a young man, I got a car. While I still had a bike, to be honest, it wasn't a major interest of mine. In fact, right up to my 40s I barely cycled at all.

But that all changed when I stumbled on small-wheeled recumbent pedal trikes – amazing machines that are incredible fun to ride. My wife Georgina loved them as well, and, in fact, for a few years was an agent for Greenspeed – makers of some of the best recumbent trikes in the world. I became fascinated with recumbent trikes, and went on to build and ride three of my own designs.

Greenspeed were then also sellers of Brompton folding bikes, and I can remember my astonishment when Georgina first brought a Brompton home and demonstrated its folding ability. I love engineering, and the Greenspeed trikes and Brompton bikes are engineering masterpieces – so apparently simple, but so effective in design.

Owning folding Bromptons took cycling to another plane – it was so simple to take a bike along with you, whether that was on a train, in a car, or on an aircraft. We flew our Bromptons to distant places, touring on them through the countryside. I took a Brompton with me on business trips, relishing the freedom of having a magical bicycle that appeared out of a suitcase.

I did some touring on my recumbent trikes, and we also bought a pair of Birdy bikes – small-wheeled machines that fold and have full front and rear suspension. Then I found an old Moulton that needed a full restoration – and suddenly realised that we seemed to have a plethora of small-wheel bikes around the place! It wasn't planned – it just seemed to happen …

So why the book? I think that many people are completely unaware of the advantages of small-wheeled bikes – bikes that would suit them so well. From nipping down to the shops to pick up some groceries, to touring across a country, to taking a bike

Small-wheeled pedal machines – a better way of cycling

for day rides when you go on holiday – all can be so easily achieved with small-wheeled bikes.

Building and restoring pedal machines, and riding such a variety of different bikes and trikes, has also made me think that much advice that is given to prospective cyclists is wrong. Of all the people who ride – or want to ride – bikes, only a small proportion are hard-core, super-fit cyclists. And yet much of the available advice on bikes is written by people of that ilk. The result is that many people try bikes that for them are wrongly geared and uncomfortable – and the result of *that* is a rather short-lived enthusiasm for riding!

Especially with small-wheeled bikes, it's easy to buy a bike that will not achieve what you want from it. That's why in this book I've dedicated a lot of space to talking about selecting a bike that suits *you* – your type of usage, your strength and fitness, and your tolerance of bumps. When the difference between struggling miserably up hills – or easily climbing them – is just the gearing that has been selected for the bike, you can soon see how important these decisions are.

It's also false economy to buy cheaply. A good small-wheeled machine won't be low in cost – but it will be well-designed, durable, effective and have good retained value. A quality bike, maintained appropriately, will have a long life – 10 or even 20 years. That initial outlay starts to look pretty good when you spread the cost over that time frame.

If you already ride a small-wheeled pedal machine, I'm probably talking to the converted – and I hope that you'll see this book as more of a celebration of what we both know. If you ride a conventional bike and wonder about small-wheeled machines, welcome. There's a world of advantages you can discover!

Acknowledgements

My thanks to those companies that made photographs available: Bike Friday, Brompton Bicycle, Greenspeed, HP Velotechnik and the Moulton Bicycle Company. Individuals who contributed photographs and other information were Stephen Nurse, Brian Perkins, Josephine O'Brien, Brian Walsh, Dan Farrell, and Connie and Jurien Dekter. Thanks to all these generous people.

Out for a day ride on a Moulton. (Courtesy Brian Perkins)

Chapter 1

Design

This book is about small-wheeled cycling machines – a tiny minority of all bicycles. In fact, of the 130 million bicycles that are sold each year, in relative terms only a mere handful of them have small wheels. Look at events like the Tour de France – there's not even *one* small-wheeled bike participating! So why on earth would you want to ride a small-wheeled cycling machine? Clearly, they can't be much good …

Well, did you know that small-wheeled machines are banned in almost all competitive cycling events? That's right; even if you wanted to, you couldn't use a small-wheeled bike in the Olympics, or in the Tour de France – or in most mainstream bicycle sporting events you can think of. The Union Cycliste Internationale (UCI) rules state that the bikes used must have wheels with a minimum diameter of 550mm (21.7in). Furthermore, the wheels must be of equal diameter, and other rules relating to frame dimensions prevent the use of recumbent bikes (designs where the pedals are in front of you, rather than below you). In fact, recumbents were outlawed way back in 1934!

To put that into a rather interesting context, most of the outright fastest bikes in the world use small wheels. How fast? These are the machines that can travel at over 130km/h (~80mph) on pedal power alone – and without drafting (slipstreaming). The small wheels allow the frontal area of the streamlined machines to be reduced, so lowering wind resistance. I'd love to see more mainstream competitions where people could ride whatever they like, so long as propulsion was via human power alone. And if that occurred, small-wheeled bikes would become much more common – you can be sure of that.

So, now that we've put aside the fallacy that small-wheeled bikes are slow, let's look at some of the other major advantages that small-wheeled machines have over their large-wheeled brethren. And then, to be fair, I'll also look at some of the disadvantages of having small wheels.

Advantages of small wheels
More space available over both wheels
If the wheels are smaller, there is more space available above the wheels.

To see this, consider a front luggage basket on a bike. On a typical bike with full-size wheels, the basket can be about 200mm high x 400mm wide and 200mm deep (about 8 x 16 x 8in). If we move that same basket to a bike with 16-inch wheels, the basket's width and depth remain unchanged – but at 400mm (16in), the height can be literally twice as great. So you can store 100 per cent more luggage on the front of the bike, without going wider or deeper! A similar situation exists at the back of the bike, over the rear wheel. And in addition to the greater carrying volume available, the weight

A small-wheeled bike has more space available over both the front and back wheels. This also positions the extra weight closer to the centreline of the bike, making balance easier. Note how the frame design of this Bike Friday leaves room for two drinks bottles – and one of these is huge. (Courtesy Bike Friday)

is positioned over the bike centreline, rather than hanging off the side as is common with side-mount panniers, improving weight distribution and reducing wind resistance.

The smaller wheels also allow the adjustment range of the seat and handlebars to be greater. There's more clearance, and so adjusting these downwards doesn't cause clashes with the frame components holding the wheels. The smaller wheels also make it easier to produce step-through frame designs. In turn, these two factors mean that a single small-wheeled bike design can be unisex, and fit a wide variety of people – from tall to short.

Easier to incorporate suspension

Small wheels give more room for incorporating suspension. (Now this is rather lucky, because bikes with small wheels are more likely to need suspension – something covered later in this chapter.) Bikes with suspension have better ride quality (you feel bumps and road harshness less) and better roadholding (the grip on the road is improved, especially over bumps).

Small wheels take up less space

The smaller wheels mean that the bicycle's length is shorter – even if the wheelbase (the distance between the axles) is the same as the big-wheel bike. The difference in overall length between a large and small wheel bike can be considerable – for example 230mm (9in). With the wheels taking up less space, the bike design can also be more flexible – for example, the wheelbase can be longer or shorter than normal, or the bike can be configured as a recumbent.

Small wheels are lighter

Smaller wheels are lighter than larger wheels. That's the case when they're measured on a set of bathroom scales, but even more interestingly, that weight also has an important impact when they are spinning.

A lighter wheel has what is called a reduced 'moment of inertia.' You can think of this as the amount of energy required to spin the wheel up to speed. The heavier the weight, and the further that weight is located outwards from the axle, the greater the effort to increase the speed of the wheel – and also to slow it down. This means that it's easier to accelerate and brake a small-wheeled bike.

On bikes with suspension, the parts that move up and down (the wheels and forks) need to be as light as possible compared with the rest of the bike. Taking this approach allows the suspension to work well, with the tyres following the road surface over bumps, but the rest of the bike not moving much vertically. Smaller – and so lighter – wheels help achieve this.

Small wheels have lower wind resistance

We've all felt how much harder it is to ride into a headwind. This is because air resistance forms a large proportion of the effort we need to overcome with our pedalling legs, especially when going fast. Anything that reduces air resistance is therefore a good thing, and a smaller diameter wheel poses less air resistance than a large one. This is the case for two reasons: the smaller wheel has a reduced frontal area (the height and width facing into the airflow) and the shorter spokes are pushing into less air as the wheels spins. Incidentally, the shorter spokes also allow the wheel to be made stronger for its weight.

Small wheels on a pedal machine have major advantages – but they also have some disadvantages. Understanding both is important before you pick a small-wheeled bike. (Courtesy Brompton)

Wheels have smaller diameter

The smaller the diameter of the wheel, the less strain there is on the driving hub. For example, in hubs with internal gears (eg the classic 3-speed), the forces are smaller if the wheel size is less. If a hub or disc brake is being used, it is also more effective on smaller wheels. Smaller wheels also allow the use of shorter (easier) gearing, if required. And for those touring long distances, smaller wheels in turn mean smaller spare tyres (and tubes) to carry.

That's a formidable list of advantages – but what are the disadvantages of small wheels on bikes?

Disadvantages of small wheels
Small wheels are lighter

Hold on, didn't I just list 'wheels are lighter' as an advantage? Well, it's both an advantage *and* a disadvantage.

The lighter wheel has a smaller moment of inertia, and in turn this reduces the gyroscopic effect of the spinning wheel. (The gyroscopic effect is best felt when you have a wheel off the bike. Hold the axle by each end, with the wheel orientated vertically as it is on the bike. Now have someone give the wheel a hefty spin, and then try to steer the spinning wheel. You will immediately feel this odd force resisting your steering movements – and in fact causing movements in other directions.)

The reduced gyroscopic effect of small wheels doesn't, as you might first think, have a major impact on the ease, or otherwise, of keeping the bike upright. However, you lose some of the effect where, as you turn into the corner, the spinning wheel helps you turn further (this is called 'gyroscopic precession') and it makes the steering less damped (more likely to shake) and change direction – it is this last factor that makes a small-wheeled bike much harder to steer 'no-hands.'

Wheel hub contamination

With the wheel hubs nearer the ground, it's easier for them to get contaminated with water and dirt. (Of course, the answer to this is easy – use sealed bearings and/or keep water and dirt shields in good condition.)

Wheels have smaller diameter

Wheel diameter is another one that makes its way into both the 'advantages' and 'disadvantages' sections. The smaller diameter of the wheel makes rim braking (eg using conventional caliper brakes) less effective. This is because the retarding force is closer to the axle, and so there is less leverage. Higher gears are also harder to achieve. Because the final 'gear' (the diameter of the wheel) is less, higher gearing needs to be used ahead of it – for example, using a larger front cog. (A popular misconception is that small-wheeled bikes are always going to be geared lower than large wheel bikes, but this is simply not the case.)

However, the major disadvantage of the smaller diameter wheels is higher rolling resistance. A smaller diameter tyre sinks more deeply into a soft surface, and if everything else remains the same, a smaller diameter tyre has greater rolling resistance on any surface. However, the key phrase is 'if everything else remains the same' – because it doesn't! If high tyre pressures are used, rolling resistance is similar – or even lower – than with large wheels. But the use

of high pressures, and the fact that smaller wheels find every pebble a bigger hill to climb, and every hole an easier one to fall into, means that the use of suspension becomes important.

Some of the small-wheeled bikes of the Sixties and Seventies used balloon-type tyres inflated to low pressures. To save money, no suspension was fitted – the low-pressure tyres performing the same function. However, the rolling resistance of the low-pressure tyres was very high – so with lots of pedalling effort required to get anywhere, these bikes developed a poor reputation.

So ...

So with small-wheeled bikes having both technical advantages and disadvantages, how does the ledger look?

For bikes that are used on roads and paths by people who want to carry things, and who want to be able to easily store their bike when it is not being used, small-wheeled machines are the pick. Add to those positives the fact that some small-wheeled bikes can be folded (or disassembled) into tiny packages – as in, small enough to fit in a suitcase – and the list of positives just grows. I also like the idea that small wheels lend themselves to innovative pedal machine designs like recumbent trikes – and even the development of fully-enclosed velomobiles.

But as we saw with the description of the small-wheel, balloon tyre, low-cost bikes of the Seventies, it's also possible to take a concept and wreck it! The key is to use high-pressure tyres with suspension. It doesn't mean that all small-wheeled bikes must have suspension, but it does mean that to achieve the very best riding outcomes, suspension is important. I'd like now to look at this topic in more detail.

Small-wheeled bike suspension

Small-wheeled bikes place unique demands on suspension. Unlike large-wheeled mountain bikes, that have suspension designed to cope with off-road rocky ground, jumps and potholes, the bike suspension that we're talking about here is designed for on-road

Moulton NS Marathon. Note the sophisticated dual leading link suspension and suspended rear triangle. The Moulton uses rubber as the springing material. (Courtesy Moulton Bicycle Company)

(and on-path) surfaces. As described previously, it is also used with tyres running high pressures, and so consequently tyre-flex absorbs much less of the bump.

Suspension consists of two aspects – springing and damping. In a perfect system, the spring absorbs the bump, preventing it being directly transmitted to the frame, and so rider. It stores that energy, and then releases it only slowly. However, all sprung systems have a disconcerting characteristic – they like to bounce. To prevent a sprung system from bouncing up and down after it has been excited, the suspension system also needs damping.

It's easy for all this to start sounding difficult, but it isn't. Get a plastic ruler and tape a weight to one end. Anchor the other end on a flat surface like a table, with the weighted end hanging in space. Now, push the weighted end down and then release it. The ruler will act as a leaf spring and the weighted end will bounce up and down. Over time the bouncing will die away, but it might take a while to stop bouncing. Now, place a hand so that the moving weight rubs against it as it bounces. The bouncing will stop more quickly, because you've added damping.

All good suspension systems must therefore incorporate both springing and damping elements. Springs used in small-wheeled bicycle suspension system are usually made of rubber cylinders or blocks, or steel coils. Damping? Glad you asked – because some bikes don't have much! Typically, it is either provided by friction (just like your hand rubbing against the weight on the bouncing ruler) or, in some cases, by a specific fluid damper like those used in car suspension (Moulton rear suspension uses fluid movement within the rubber spring).

We've established that small-wheeled bike suspension needs both springs and dampers. But what makes a suspension system effective? There are two further aspects.

The first is travel – that is, how far the wheel can move up and down. Imagine a bike has a front wheel suspension travel of just 3mm ($\frac{1}{8}$in). If you ride over a piece of gravel any larger than this, the suspension will not be able to absorb the bump. (However, even this much suspension travel will take away the harshness of riding over coarse bitumen.) A suspension travel of only 3mm ($\frac{1}{8}$in) is tiny, so let's increase it by ten times to 30mm ($1\frac{3}{16}$in). You can immediately see that a much larger bump will be absorbed – and that's good. Therefore, longer suspension travel is a good thing.

However, the travel doesn't tell you how soft the spring is. The best way of ascertaining this is to see how much the suspension compresses when you place your weight on the bike. This is a really important aspect of suspension design, and so is even given its own name – 'static deflection.' The less the static deflection, typically the harder the ride.

If you sit on a bike and the static deflection is minimal, there could be two reasons for that – neither good! The first is that the springing is really stiff, and the second is that the damping is too strong. So just by sitting on the bike, and without riding anywhere, you

can get a feel for how effective the suspension will or won't be. A good suspension system will compress by 30-50 per cent of its full travel when you sit on the bike, and when you bounce up and down on the seat, the bounces will quickly die away.

Now – what about pedalling? Here's where the challenges facing the bike suspension designer become acute. Remember the ruler and weight that bounced up and down? So how fast was it bouncing? Let's say that the weight bounced up and down twice a second – 120 times a minute. (This characteristic is another given a special name – it's called the 'natural frequency' of the system.)

To be effective at absorbing bumps, many bike suspension systems have a natural frequency in the 90-120 bounces per minute range. The trouble is, that's also potentially close to your cadence (cadence is the number of times per minute you are rotating the pedals.) So, you may be pushing down on the pedals at just the same rate the suspension naturally likes bouncing. The result? Suspension bounce, bounce, bounce. Aaah, you say, there won't be a problem – just add more damping. But then the ride will get hard!

You can see the dilemma, one that is actually best addressed by a recumbent machine, where the pedalling effort is forwards, and not up and down.

Bicycle suspension, especially on small-wheeled machines, is a complex engineering challenge that is difficult to solve, especially at a low price. But it's not impossible, and there are many ways of devising a solution.

From a buying perspective, the first point is to ensure there is adequate static deflection. If you sit on the bike and you cannot feel the suspension compress at all, there is a problem. That might be because you're a light person and the designer has specified the springing for a heavier rider. In some bikes, fitting softer suspension (eg a softer rubber bush) to cater for this change in rider weight is straightforward. In other bikes, it is not.

Second, ensure that there is adequate damping. The easiest way to assess this is to ride the bike, pedalling in a rhythmic way and see if the bike bounces fiercely. Very occasionally on small-wheeled machines the suspension damping can be adjusted – but usually it cannot.

If you are going to be carrying large loads, also keep this mind when assessing suspension. A larger load will compress the suspension more (ie giving more static deflection, and so effectively a softer ride) but if you then run out of suspension travel over the biggest bump, your bike has just turned into a non-suspension bike!

Above, I talked about bouncing suspension, especially at, or near, the suspension's natural frequency. One way to avoid exciting the suspension in this way is to pedal very smoothly. This is most easily achieved by using clip-in pedals (that need special cycling shoes) or toe clips. Either approach allows you to pull up on the pedals as well as push down, so giving a smoother input of power. Having a sufficiently wide gear range that you can always maintain the same cadence, and using shorter cranks, will help with smooth power transmission.

In fact, on a small-wheeled bike, gearing is so important that it deserves its own section – so let's look at that now.

Gearing

Gearing is one of the most critical aspects of cycling to get right. I am sure that many people who would otherwise be enthusiastic cyclists are not, because the bikes that they've ridden have been geared wrongly for them. After all, if you're always in bottom gear and so struggle mightily to get up hills, there's something wrong with the bike – not you!

Partly because of the way the bike has evolved from the (very) large-wheeled penny-farthing, and partly because technical enthusiasts love using obscure language, bike gearing can seem terribly complex. So let's start by taking a different approach.

The easiest way of thinking about bike gearing is to consider *how far the bike travels forward with one complete turn of the pedals*. In a low (or 'easy') gear, the bike travels only a short distance with each pedal

turn. In a high (or 'hard') gear the bike travels much further with each turn of the pedals. Now, how fast are the pedals being turned? This preference varies for individual riders, but for many riders, the cadence at which they're happiest is about 80-90 revolutions per minute. (On a bike you should always 'windmill,' rather than strain and push at a low pedalling rate. Fast pedalling is more energy-efficient and also saves your knees from injury.)

If we know how far the bike travels forward each pedal rotation, and we know how fast the pedals are being rotated, it's easy to see how fast you'll go in each gear. So, on a flat road, without wind, how fast do *you* like going? A cyclist who loves the exercise – that's why they ride a bike – might like to travel at 25km/h (~15mph) in these conditions. Someone who likes to just potter down to the shop to buy a few groceries, and occasionally ride on that lovely cycle path to the local library, might like to ride at 15km/h (~9mph). Of course, neither preference is wrong – but it indicates the need for quite different gearing.

I suggest that when your bike has multiple gears (as all small-wheeled bikes should), *you should be in the middle gear of the range, at your natural preferred riding pace on flat ground without wind.* When you think about it, this makes perfect sense. If you are riding a bike and you are never in the highest gear, that gear is being wasted. Ditto if you're never in the lowest gear (but that's much rarer – I think many bikes are over-geared.)

Let's put some gearing figures to what we have been describing. The distance the bike travels forward for each turn of the pedals is called 'gear metres of development' and, as the name suggests, is measured in metres.

If you have a bike available, get a tape measure and go out and measure your bike's development. Place a line on the ground, and put the leading edge of the front tyre on that line. Rotate the pedals exactly one turn, driving the bike forward, then measure from the line to the new position of the leading edge of the tyre on the ground, in metres. Easy, huh?

You can then do it in each gear the bike has. On

Small-wheeled pedal machines – a better way of cycling

my standard 6-speed Brompton the results are:

Gear	Development (metres)
1	2.64
2	3.25
3	4.14
4	5.09
5	6.49
6	7.98

So in first gear on the Brompton, at my preferred cadence of 80rpm, my speed is (80 x 2.64 =) 211 metres per minute, which when multiplied by 60 gives 12,660 metres per hour – or just over 12.6km/h (about 8mph). Let's now work it out for the other gears, again using a cadence of 80rpm, and rounded to the nearest whole number.

Gear	Development (metres)	Speed at cadence of 80rpm
1	2.64	13km/h (8mph)
2	3.25	16km/h (10mph)
3	4.14	20km/h (12mph)
4	5.09	24km/h (15mph)
5	6.49	31km/h (19mph)
6	7.98	38km/h (24mph)

Looking at the table, this gearing is simply too high for me. Why do I say that? Well, I just like pottering along, enjoying the experience and not being in a huge hurry to get anywhere. That translates to a

Bike manufacturers have to gear their bikes for a wide spread of potential riders. But as the purchaser of a bike, you don't have to. Instead, you can specify the gearing to match your pedalling rate and your natural speed on the flat. Doing this makes a radical difference to the usability of your bike. (Courtesy Brompton)

A fit, powerful cyclist can work with gearing much higher than a rather unfit cyclist, who just wants to enjoy an ambling ride. Neither approach is wrong – but each approach needs bike gearing that is specified to suit. (Courtesy Bike Friday)

cruising speed of about 12-15km/h (about 7-9mph). In turn, looking at the table, that means I am very often in 1st or 2nd gears – at a cadence of 80rpm, they give 13 and 16km/h respectively. (Therefore, and this is important, there are *no lower gears available* to climb hills or assist when I have a load aboard!)

At the other extreme, I can think of only one time ever on the Brompton when I was genuinely using 6th gear. I remember the time well, because I was on a busy, narrow urban road full of trucks and buses, and the road was heading slightly downhill – and I had a tail-wind. I decided that the safest bet was to

travel as fast as the traffic, and I remember pedalling dementedly – probably at a cadence of 100rpm in 6th gear. That in turn would translate to about 48km/h (30mph) – and it felt all of that!

To put this another way, you can see that the Brompton is geared for the most common speed, being (at a cadence of 80rpm) around 20km/h (12mph) – that's what it does in 3rd gear.

Now let's draw a contrast. Jamie, a friend of mine, says that he normally (no wind, flat road conditions) travels on his bike at 35km/h (22mph). At his chosen cadence of 90rpm (so higher than my 80), he will need gearing that gives his bike a development of about 6.5 metres – remember, that is 6.5 metres of forward travel per revolution of the pedals.

Now you can see the dilemma for the bicycle manufacturer – and why Brompton has selected the gearing it has. Looking at the previous table, I will be in 1st or 2nd gears, but Jamie will be 5th or 6th – so that's great, there is a gear ratio suitable for both of us. However, when *you* are selecting a bike, you don't have to worry about the Julians and the Jamies of this world – you only need to worry about yourself.

So, the first rule is to select a gearing that puts *you* in the middle gear of the range, with a displacement that suits your average riding speed at your preferred cadence. That is:

Cadence (rpm) x displacement (metres) x 60 ÷ 1000 = km/h

or

km/h x 1000 ÷ 60 ÷ cadence = displacement in metres

(Note: km/h divided by 1.61 = mph, and mph x 1.61 = km/h)

The next step is to consider how much higher and lower gearing than this middle ratio will be available. For example, take a 5-speed Sturmey Archer internal hub. The gear ratios that are available can be expressed like this:

Gear	Percentage
1	63
2	75
3	100
4	133
5	160

This is a good way of showing it, because you can see that the near-middle gear (3rd) is tagged at 100 – that is, 100 per cent.

Let's say that we have organised the gearing for my snail-like pace, and we want 100 per cent (3rd gear) to therefore equal a development of 3.1 metres, or at

80rpm cadence, near enough to 15km/h (9mph). I've put this number in the table below.

Gear	Percentage	Speed at cadence of 80rpm
1	63	
2	75	
3	100	15km/h (9mph)
4	133	
5	160	

Now what will be the speeds in the other gears? The percentage variation gives you a clue. If first gear is 63 per cent of 3rd gear, then 63 per cent of 15 (63/100 x 15) = 9.45, rounded down to 9km/h. You can do the other numbers in the same way.

Gear	Percentage	Speed at cadence of 80rpm
1	63	9km/h (6mph)
2	75	11km/h (7mph)
3	100	15km/h (9mph)
4	133	20km/h (12mph)
5	160	24km/h (15mph)

A 4-speed internal hub in a restored Moulton Mark I. (Courtesy Brian Perkins)

For me, this gearing is now looking really good! On a flat surface without any wind, I'll be doing 15km/h (9mph) in 3rd gear. Maintaining the same cadence, I can drop that to 9km/h (6mph) in first gear to climb hills, or go as fast as 24km/h (15mph) in 5th gear down hills or with a big tail-wind. Jamie would hate it – but I'd love it.

Not that the speeds shown in the above table are all at my preferred 80rpm cadence. To put this another way, if your pedalling rate drops greatly on hills and into headwinds, it's because you don't have a low enough gear available.

At this point, you can simply go to a bicycle shop and say; "I would like the bike configured so that it has a development of 'X' metres in the middle gear," and leave them to work out how to achieve that. This approach saves you having to worry about wheel sizes, front cog sizes, rear cog sizes and internal hub ratios. And it's perfectly reasonable to let someone else do that work.

Selecting gear componentry

If you want to delve into the next level of specifying components, or if you find that your shop doesn't understand 'metres displacement,' you'll need to know about 'gear inches.' Incredibly, this method of describing bike gearing dates back to penny-farthing bicycles – and it is still very commonly used. This number refers to how far a bike would move forward if its driving wheel were the diameter of the gear-inches number. Thus, on a bicycle geared at 72 gear inches, one revolution of the pedals would advance the bicycle the same distance that a 72-inch wheel would in one revolution. To say this is a bizarre way of describing gearing is an understatement – which is why I haven't introduced it until now.

To convert gear inches to metres of displacement, multiply by 0.08. (To convert from metres of displacement, divide by 0.08.) Let's look at an example. It's for the Sturmey Archer 5-speed internal hub, when it is being used on a bike with 16-inch wheels.

Front cog (number of teeth)	Rear cog (number of teeth)	1st	2nd	3rd	4th	5th
44	13	35	42	56	75	90
	14	33	39	52	69	83
	15	30	36	49	65	78
	16	28	34	46	61	73

Remember that these figures are in gear-inches, not metres displacement. The overall gear ratio of the 5-speed hub is determined by the number of teeth on the front cog and the number of teeth on the rear cog – and here there are four different rear cog options, from 13 to 16 teeth.

I want to travel at 15km/h (9mph) in 3rd gear, which at my chosen cadence is a development of 3.07 metres. To convert to gear-inches we divide by 0.08, which gives a figure of 38.4 gear-inches. Looking at the table, this shows what a snail I am – I need the largest rear cog (16 teeth) and even then, I'll probably be more often in 2nd gear (34 gear-inches) than 3rd (46 gear-inches)!

Gearing range

So far, I have been talking about the overall gearing of the bike, and how you should match the middle gear with your cadence and preferred speed on the flat. But there's another aspect of gearing that is important to consider. What is the ratio of the highest to lowest gear – in other words, how wide is the gearing spread? If you divide the highest gear ratio (expressed as either metres development or gear-inches) by the lowest, you'll see the range available.

For example, if the highest gear is 73 gear-inches, and the lowest is 28 gear-inches, 73/28 = 2.6; that is, the highest gear is 2.6 times the lowest. This is typical of a 5-speed internal hub, while a 3-speed internal hub might have a range of only 1.8 times. The 6-speed Brompton described above, that uses a 2-speed derailleur with a 3-speed hub, has a range of 3, as does the Birdy with a 9-speed rear derailleur and internal hub gears. Greater ranges than this are possible, eg by using front and rear derailleur systems

Changing gearing for special trips

Sometimes, you want a range of gearing that suits your normal bike use – and *another* range of gearing that suits more difficult conditions.

For example, let's say that you normally ride your bike largely unladen and on flat roads. The gearing you have selected matches this very well. But then let's imagine that you want to go on a cycle touring holiday, loaded with panniers and pulling a trailer. Now you want gearing that is much lower.

The easiest way of achieving this is to simply swap to a smaller front cog, and adjust the chain length to suit.

This approach is simple, cheap and effective. (On an internal hub system, you could also swap to a smaller rear cog, or on a derailleur system to a smaller rear cluster.) You can do it yourself, but if you don't think you have the ability, any bike shop will do it at nominal charge.

Common front cog sizes include 44, 50 and 54 teeth. But since the larger the front cog, the higher the gearing, you will want to go for something smaller. Mountain bike cranksets with 40, 30 or 22 teeth match that requirement for a reduced size front cog.

To work out how much lower the gearing will be, look at the percentage reduction in teeth number. If you currently have a 44 tooth front cog, a new front cog with (say) 30 teeth will drop all the gears by 32 per cent (44 – 30 = 14, 14 ÷ 44 = 0.32, 0.32 x 100 = 32) – plenty for pulling big loads!

If the bike has a chain tensioner (eg Brompton, Birdy – or other bikes with a rear derailleur) you may find that you can fit dual front cog wheels, and then manually swap the chain over when conditions require a lower or higher gear. (To do this, stop the bike, then use a stick to move the chain over while pedalling backwards.)

Cycle touring with a Brompton 6-speed and a child trailer carrying a 2-year-old and plenty of gear. I fitted a twin front cog that could be manually changed when the grades got too steep. The standard Brompton chain tensioner coped with this, though the chain came off when the bike was folded – not often on this trip. (Courtesy Georgina Edgar)

(5:1) and even higher ranges again can be gained by using front/rear derailleur systems with internal hubs – this is often done with recumbent touring trikes.

Lighting and being seen

It's important on all bikes that you are seen by other road users. That's even more the case on a small-wheeled cycling machine – whether that is a bike or recumbent trike. So how do you achieve this? The cheapest, lowest energy way is to wear bright colours, and have a brightly-coloured machine.

Hi-visibility tops are available in a wide range of weights – from singlets through to padded jackets. Clothing with sewn-in reflective stripes (3M Scotchlite is still the best) will work from dusk conditions through to absolute darkness – so long as the drivers of other vehicles have lights. Large reflectors will make you much more visible, and if the reflectors are moving, so much the better. This includes reflectors on pedals, wheel spokes and even pedalling legs. Buying a few metres (yards) of good quality reflecting tape and adding strategically-placed pieces to your pedalling machine is cheap insurance.

The other important aspect is lighting. Thankfully, cycle lighting has undergone a revolution in recent years with the advent of high power, low current consumption LED lighting. Depending on the country that you live in, that lighting might be flashing or static, but in either case, you should aim to have 'see-me' lighting facing to the rear, sides and forwards. (Note that many people forget the 'side' aspect.) To see

where you are going requires another type of lighting – bright, and with a carefully-focused beam.

I must admit to being a bit unfashionable: I am a real fan of hub dynamo lighting. A typical hub dynamo lighting system is rated at 6V/3W – a hangover from the filament bulbs of the past. This much power will not allow you, for example, to run a 5W headlight, a headlight power commonly available from USB-style 5V lithium-ion battery packs. As a result, if you are using a hub dynamo, you will be limited to lower power lights. However, the huge advantage of hub dynamo systems is that they never get flat batteries, and so they can be on all the time.

I always liked the idea of a hub dynamo, but when I bought my Brompton equipped with such a system, I became completely convinced. Suddenly, lights were no longer the hassle they always seemed to be with battery lights. No more recharging, no more replacement batteries – just get on the bike and ride. You don't even need to remember to switch them on

A SON hub dynamo fitted to a Brompton. Hub dynamos never get flat batteries or need recharging! (Courtesy Brompton)

(just leave them on all the time), and a good system will make you more visible, without any extra effort felt in pedalling. I've lost count of the number of times that people have commented on my lighting in day time – and I've forgotten the lighting is even on. On my rebuilt Moulton (see Chapter 7) I use a Shutter Precision front hub dynamo and a capacitor-based storage system.

Also note that you can use the hub dynamo lighting as a back-up. That is, add a more powerful battery-operated light (eg another headlight) and then be assured that even if the battery in that light suddenly dies, you'll always have lighting on display. If you are buying a new bike that is being built to your specifications, and you can afford the extra cost, I highly recommend hub dynamo lighting.

Chapter 2

Fixed-frame bikes

As we've seen, small-wheeled bikes have major advantages over bikes with conventional large wheels. But how did small-wheeled bikes happen? One man was largely responsible for the change – Alex Moulton. And his company still makes small-wheeled bikes like this one – perhaps the best in the world. (Courtesy Moulton Bicycle Company)

Small-wheeled pedal machines – a better way of cycling

We've already seen that small-wheeled pedal machines have major advantages over conventional, large-wheeled bikes. One advantage is their smaller size for storage or transport – and so those bikes that fold have an immediate advantage. However, many people choose to ride fixed-frame small-wheeled bikes, for the advantages they have in carrying goods and their responsiveness. In this chapter I'll cover fixed-frame bikes, and in the next chapter, bikes that fold.

Fixed-frame, small-wheeled bikes are also interesting because they unexpectedly appeared about 55 years ago – well after the advent of the traditional large-wheeled bike. With any well-developed technology, sudden change is very unusual. Instead, the normal progression is subtle, incremental – and not something dramatic! So what actually happened to bring about this radical new design?

The genesis of small-wheeled biking – the Moulton

As the motor car came within reach of ordinary people, cycle use in the UK declined. In the 1950s, this decline seemed terminal. Bicycles were unfashionable; yesterday's mode of transport. The car was king. But during the first Suez crisis in 1956, fuel was rationed in the UK – so perhaps this future full of shiny cars and endless tarmac roads was not assured … or at least not on a ration of 320km (200mi) of petrol a month!

A man in Wiltshire was troubled by this restriction and bought himself a lightweight bicycle – a Hetchins – as, in his own words, "a serious alternative means of locomotion." He found a 'revelation of joy' in riding this, but also thought it a little cumbersome, and found carrying his briefcase difficult. But his interest was piqued. He would later say, "I rode it thoughtfully, inviting it to speak to me." He resolved to improve on it.

This man was Alex Moulton. Bicycles had featured in Moulton's mind before – he'd approached Raleigh with a design for bicycle suspension as early as 1948. But this was different. Moulton's intent in 1960 was to make a bicycle that was:

Alex Moulton pictured on one of his early production bikes.
(Courtesy Moulton Bicycle Company)

○ more convenient and pleasing
○ suitable for all the family
○ easy to lift, stow and park, with provision for carrying things on it.

Remember, at the time, no mass-production bicycle met all these criteria. None!

Moulton questioned everything, including riding position. However, he concluded that the conventional riding position was optimal. He also queried the apparent necessity for large wheels, and decided that the reasons for the large wheels were irrelevant in post-war Britain.

(He had seen his friend and collaborator Alec

Issigonis do the same thing in automotive circles – first with the Morris Minor and then later with the Mini – both of which used small wheels, the Mini staggeringly so.)

However, his first data on efficiency of small wheels came from aircraft undercarriages, one of the few areas where low rolling resistance is as important as on a bicycle.

Moulton decided that the new design of bicycle should have:

○ small wheels
○ suspension front and rear
○ a low, step-through frame with adjustability provided through the seat pillar and handlebar stem.

However, the first design direction – using sheet aluminium to produce a monocoque – was not successful. Moulton later recalled that he had created this terrible thing – a noisy bicycle – and this started the move towards tubular construction used on all subsequent Moulton bikes. While Moulton's first designs also didn't have suspension, he soon realised that it was highly desirable for ride comfort and road-holding.

Moulton never intended to make bicycles himself, so he approached Raleigh to do so. Raleigh was a hugely dominant cycle company in the UK that had absorbed almost all of their competitors, and had then recently merged with Tube Investments (TI). Raleigh was initially very interested, but eventually decided not to go ahead with the radical new bike, due to concern over its financial viability. There was a nervousness by all about the small wheels; no-one really knew how people would react. Small-wheeled adult bikes were completely uncharted territory.

So, in 1962, Moulton built a new factory and launched his bicycle – as it proved, with great success. The story goes that on the first day of the Earl's Court show in 1962, Moulton spoke to the firm building his new factory and ordered it to be doubled in size. Later in the week, George Harriman, Managing Director of BMC, told Alex not to hesitate to take orders as the British Motor Corporation (BMC) would make the

The first rideable prototype of the Moulton bicycle with monocoque construction, the 'noisy bicycle.'
(Courtesy Moulton Bicycle Company)

bikes for him. Today, that would be like Ford or Toyota offering to make your bicycles!

Impact

So what impact did this radical new design have? Remember that, back in 1962, nobody had previously seen anything like the Moulton bike. In fact, everybody was amazed that the diamond frame bicycle design – a design that seemed perfect from a functional point of view – could be improved upon.

But as we've seen, Alex Moulton thought differently about big-wheeled bicycles, recognising their limitations. Conventional bicycles were difficult to mount and dismount. The wheels were cumbersome and easily buckled. It was difficult to carry loads safely and easily, and carriers were always a bolted-on afterthought, not designed-in. Socially, bicycles had a serious image problem, being associated with poverty and lacking in stylish appeal. In one fell swoop, the Moulton changed all of that.

The Moulton had two upright steel tubes connected by a larger diameter, rounded rectangular

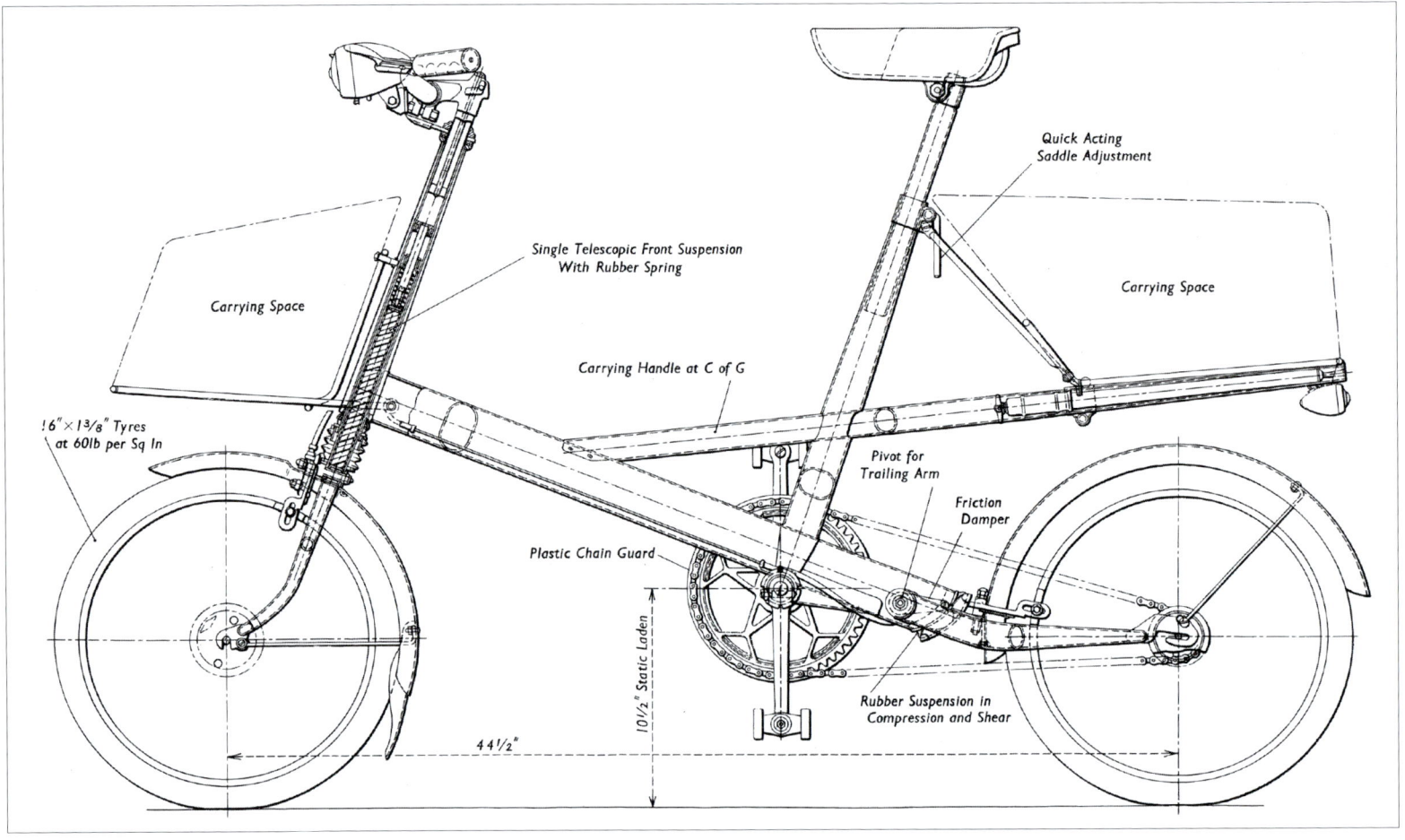

Quick Acting
Saddle Adjustment

Single Telescopic Front Suspension
With Rubber Spring

Carrying Space

Carrying Space

Carrying Handle at C of G

!6" × 1³/₈" Tyres
at 60lb per Sq In

Pivot for
Trailing Arm

Friction
Damper

Plastic Chain Guard

10¹/₂" Static Laden

Rubber Suspension in
Compression and Shear

4 4¹/₂"

Note how the front and rear carriers are integrated with the frame design, and how front and rear suspension was incorporated. The low step-through height is also obvious. (Courtesy Moulton Bicycle Company)

tube – the classic 'F' frame. It is so simple that we can easily overlook the cleverness of this solution. Moulton had consciously thrown away the conventional thinking of triangular structure to achieve his aim of creating an easy-to-mount open frame. This was a huge creative leap.

So, what else made for a breakthrough bike? Top of the list was the suspension, fitted to both front and rear. Alex Moulton was a rubber suspension innovator who designed the Austin Mini's suspension, and, with Alec Issigonis, invented the Hydrolastic system that was used on millions of cars. Moulton knew rubber, and even more importantly, he also understood that consumer products needed to be at a price that normal people could afford. He was therefore that

rarest of persons: a mechanical genius who thought in terms of price as well as mechanical prowess.

The rear suspension is both supple and subtle. It isn't made for jumping over logs or careering down mountains. It's for smoothing out the vibrations that you would find on different road surfaces. The rubber block, compressed and sheared by the rear suspension arm moving upwards, looks very simple, though it's anything but.

First, the majority of forces are fed into the end of the large diameter frame. The suspension is trying to compress this frame tube, rather than bend it. Since tubes are very strong in compression, this works very well. Second, rubber in compression has what is called a 'rising rate.' This means it gets stiffer very fast when it is compressed. In a bike, this would mean that the suspension was soft initially, and then got very hard with bigger suspension movements. To avoid this problem, Moulton designed the rear rubber spring so that the block was initially compressed, and then subsequently sheared (moved sideways). This combination of compression and shear gives a more linear (although still rising rate) rear suspension. Friction damping was provided by tightening the nuts on the rear pivot, so forcing the rear arms mounts against plastic bushes. Taking this approach was simple and allowed the damping to be adjusted.

At the front, a completely different approach is used. This time, the wheel movement upwards on bump, and the spring compression, are similar in the distance they travel – what is called a 1:1 motion ratio. The spring comprises a column of rubber surrounded by a metal spiral spring. This provides a damped ride. There is also a rebound spring to take out the clang when the forks extend.

Apart from being an excellent solution to the problem, front and rear rubber suspension was, in the 1960s, an entirely new departure for bicycle design, one which promised to marry high efficiency with higher levels of comfort. Importantly, it was this dual improvement that allowed the Moulton to be a superb sports bicycle and a comfortable utility bicycle.

The next great feature are the wheels that, at first sight, seem so incredibly dinky. Small wheels give the Moulton quick steering and nimble handling. There's no huge wheel swinging around in front or splattering mud up your back. And of course, the small wheels also create a lot of room for carrying loads.

After deciding on small diameter wheels, Alex Moulton looked at both 14-inch and 16-inch diameter tyres, and had high quality tyres to suit this wheel size constructed by Dunlop – a company he already had a close association with through his car suspension work. Immediately, it became obvious that tyre pressure was the most important influence on rolling resistance. Provided that the pressure was above 70psi, a small wheel would roll just as efficiently as a large 26-inch diameter conventional wheel. If pressure

The Moulton changed the social acceptability of cycling. Suddenly, it was fashionable – and not just for poor people. Here is a British European Airways hostess riding a Moulton in the 1960s. (Courtesy Moulton Bicycle Company)

was around 100psi, the small wheel would roll *better* than the large wheel at 70psi. Small wheels with high pressure tyres were then selected for the design.

To complete the design hat-trick, the Moulton has an 'open' frame – ie, no crossbar – which is a huge functional advantage. The ridiculous manoeuvre that you have to perform to get on the saddle of all diamond frame gent's bikes immediately became a thing of the past. (In fact, Moulton said he thought that if a diamond framed bike were to be introduced now,

Small-wheeled pedal machines – a better way of cycling

The Moulton with typical grocery-getting bags. The front suspension can be identified only by the rubber bellows, while the rear suspension mechanism is all but invisible. This bike was radical in nearly every way. (Courtesy Brian Perkins)

it would be banned – so dangerous is the high cross-bar!) Also, at the rear was a sturdy carrying platform integrated with the frame.

Moulton's frame was really revolutionary. Aircraft and automotive construction techniques were used in place of traditional lugs: it had a flatted main beam and a pierced seat tube, and there was only one small triangle in the mainframe. In construction, MIG welding and spot-welding augmented traditional bicycle brazing. But more importantly, the Moulton design looked right – even now, it looks modern and stylish.

Moulton bikes were not folders – or indeed separable. Their design was all about a better bicycle, more pleasing to own and use. 'Stowaway' (separable) models did come, partially led by the strong relationship between Moulton and BMC – a Stowaway bike could be placed in the small boot (trunk) of contemporary BMC car models.

Moulton had less than two years of 'blue ocean' for his bicycle to sink or swim. In that time, he became the second-largest single-name maker in the UK. However, as the bicycle market picked up after years of decline, others entered the small-wheel market. Among the first out of the blocks was the Dawes Newpin in 1964, closely followed by the Kingpin in 1965. This bike was certainly inspired by Moulton but was significantly different, with larger wheels and an 'H' frame layout, and was a very practical machine.

Dawes may have merely irked Alex Moulton, whereas Raleigh – or more specifically the Raleigh RSW16 – provoked more of a reaction. Raleigh were spooked both by the success of the Moulton and by BMC's involvement. TI Raleigh were the giants in the bike world, but BMC dwarfed them. Raleigh's new bicycle was much more in the image of the Moulton and was clearly a direct competitor in appearance, if not in performance. Raleigh put their full weight behind the RSW 16, including an unprecedented launch spend and some rather unsubstantiated claims including the proclamation that the RSW 16 was "the greatest advance in two-wheeled design this century." One of Alex's friends wrote a postscript on one of his letters: "I see Raleigh have launched a copycat bicycle in competition with yours. Perhaps an advertisement could be placed – "Raleigh – the almost all-steal bicycle." (Raleigh's marketing slogan was Raleigh – the all-steel bicycle.)

The upshot of all of this was that, by 1966, the small-wheel market – that hadn't even existed in early 1962 – was looking rather crowded. Also, Raleigh was the default choice of bicycle for many, and, while the RSW looked like a Moulton, it didn't go like one, and the riding experience was disappointing. Many say that the RSW was responsible for the public perception that small wheels are 'slow' or 'not serious.'

On top of this competition, Moulton was also affected by warranty issues and dealer resistance. The resulting dramatic drop in sales put Moulton and his manufacturing partner BMC into an awkward spot and in 1967, following a failure to react to drop in demand, they were massively overstocked and experiencing cashflow issues. Moulton sold out to Raleigh later that year and was retained by them as a consultant. As you might expect, the deal was an unlikely and uneasy match for both parties.

Competition

In the spirit of 'Win on Sunday, sell on Monday,' racing cyclist John Woodburn was enlisted to attempt to break the Cardiff to London distance record on a Moulton. Remember, at the time, no serious racing cyclist would even consider such a small-wheeled machine. On December 9th, 1962, Woodburn was successful, immediately putting the Moulton on the map as a serious bicycle.

John Woodburn broke the Cardiff to London cycling record on December 9, 1962. The 261km (162mi) distance was ridden in 6 hours, 43 minutes and 23 seconds – an average of nearly 39km/h (24mph). This ride showed the Moulton to be a serious speed machine. (Courtesy Moulton Bicycle Company)

While many have thought that Raleigh bought Moulton in order to kill it, this is far from the truth. Raleigh's intent with Moulton was straightforward – while the smaller Moulton Mini was acceptable in terms of production and profit, the full-size model was troublesome in both areas and needed to be redesigned as soon as possible. The resulting Moulton Mark III was launched in 1970.

In 1968, with more than a sideways glance at Dawes, and none of the fanfare of the RSW launch, Raleigh introduced the Twenty. With larger 20-inch wheels, this – like the Kingpin – was not a Moulton copy, and owed more to the Dawes model. Whichever, it was an extraordinary success, becoming the definitive 'shopper' bike. It was Raleigh's biggest seller, and at its height in 1975, it managed 140,000 sales in just that year.

One of the all-time classic cycling pictures – London and a Moulton bicycle, complete with briefcase and rider wearing a bowler hat! (Courtesy Moulton Bicycle Company)

Small-wheeled pedal machines – a better way of cycling

The Raleigh 20. As its name suggests, it used large 20-inch wheels. Despite its stylish appearance and excellent sales, it lacked innovation, and – arguably – harmed the reputation of small-wheeled bikes for the next 50 years!

So small-wheeled bikes had become popular in the UK, but they were very different in origin, technology and riding experience. You could say that the exceptional purity of the original had been so diluted, the public perception of the brilliance of small-wheeled bikes equipped with suspension was largely lost forever.

The 1970s

1970s bought a shift in the small-wheeled bicycle market, and the first real – and successful – portable bicycle, the Bickerton Portable. Harry Bickerton was an aeronautical engineer who was frustrated by how difficult combining public and personal transport was. Taking a bike on the train was, at the time, expensive. Bickerton considered many ways to get to and from the station – including roller skates – before concluding that a portable bicycle was the best option. Of course, it could also be useful for those with boats, planes, on buses – anywhere. He designed his bicycle to be as light and as small as possible.

Like Moulton, it used methods of manufacture unknown to the cycle industry. Unlike Moulton, its manufacture was not sophisticated – 'knife and fork' methods and the stove in Bickerton's kitchen were used for heat treatment. The bike used a 14-inch front wheel and a 16-inch rear. The Bickerton was astonishingly light at under 10kg. It was built of aluminium and had no welded joints. The frame folded, the handlebars folded, and it stowed into a bag. When ridden, the same bag could hang from the handlebars to carry luggage. It adjusted to suit almost anyone.

Riding a Bickerton is an unusual experience, and many cyclists find the ride unnerving. Whereas

Harry Bickerton and the Bickerton Portable bicycle, 1971. The first really successful folding bike, it paved the way for the truly stunning Brompton – covered in the next chapter. (Courtesy Mark Bickerton)

Moulton designed a stiff frame and introduced suspension to articulate the frame very precisely, Bickerton designed a bike that was strong enough to carry you, but had very little of the rigidity of a conventional machine. Harry Bickerton himself found the Bickerton bicycle "really marvellous to ride. Acceleration is amazing, hill-climbing outstanding, and the general responsiveness and performance is quite exhilarating." However author Richard Ballantine described how, if you rode a Bickerton hard, it moved under you – and "sometimes in several directions at once!" But that's not necessarily a bad thing. The ride was comfortable, the bike was light, and it folded up small. It sold by the thousands, despite its price tag – £125 in 1975.

Another man inspired by all of this was Andrew Ritchie. His aim was to create an improved compact folding bike, and he eventually succeeded in building the world's best folding bike – the Brompton – that we will meet in the next chapter.

The heritage

Although these days the original Moulton Bicycle does not appear as familiar as its inventor may have wished, it did mark a step-change in the thinking of all bicycle companies, and generated a whole industry of copycat designs. Perhaps this is why the Moulton hardly appears unusual to people today.

Alex Moulton's strength as a designer was a great ability to combine his wide engineering knowledge with his intuitive design flair, favouring a practical, no-frills approach. Despite his insistence upon high efficiency and 'function-first,' his designs do seem to have inherent beauty. Having a very rounded engineering experience and knowledge of engineering materials, he was able to pull in ideas from many other areas and use these in an entirely new way. Coupled to these qualities was a determination to persevere, despite many obstacles, technical problems, and frustrations. Overall, it is the quality of his ideas that endures, and, of course, the actual quality of the machines.

This colour scheme highlights the Moulton F-type frame that provides support for the rear carrier. The optional front carrier attached to mounts integrated into the frame. The small cross-bar improves frame stiffness and, as it is located at the centre of gravity, allows the bike to be easily carried without tipping. Note also how the head-post and seat-post are both tapered, and the main tube is a rounded rectangle in cross-section – these approaches all give strength where it is needed.
(Courtesy Brian Walsh)

Modern small-wheeled bikes

So you're all excited now about small-wheeled bikes, and like the idea of a fixed-frame design – so what's available? First, a word of warning.

Many modern small-wheeled bikes are not particularly good. For example, there are low-cost examples constructed along the lines of a folding bike – but they don't fold! Others are really children's bikes. Most do not use suspension, and to overcome this issue, some use large balloon-style tyres that have a high rolling resistance. It would be easy to ride one of these machines and decide that the whole idea of a small-wheeled bike is bad.

Other, typically much more expensive bikes, are constructed with quality cycling hardware, use stiff, well-designed frames and 16, 17 or 20-inch wheels. High-end cycles like those from Moulton use effective suspension, while others (eg from Bike Friday) use wheels at the larger end of the small-wheeled spectrum, and do not have suspension. Some of these bikes are separable. (A separable bike is one that easily pulls to pieces to allow it to be packed into a small volume – eg a suitcase.) Another quality maker that has in the past produced separable small-wheeled bikes is Dahon – best known for their folders.

Of course, if you're on a budget, you can also look at buying an older fixed-frame bike and then restoring it. The 1960s Moultons are still among the best to choose – they have quality suspension, excellent frame design and good parts availability and support. I cover the restoration of my Moulton Mk1 in Chapter 7.

(Sections of this chapter are based on material prepared by Dan Farrell and Brian Perkins, and are used with permission.)

Chapter 3
Folding bikes

Folding small-wheeled bikes have a host of wonderful advantages over conventional large-wheel bikes. However, they also have some disadvantages. Let's start off by looking at the pros and cons, and then explore some folding bike options. Note that unlike the small number of fixed frame (and separable) small-wheel bikes covered in the previous chapter, there's a multitude of folding bikes available.

than a conventional bike with large wheels. For example, if you live in a small apartment, you can easily place a folding bike behind a lounge chair, in the bathroom or even under your desk. Even if you have access to a full-size garage, but that space is cluttered, you can still find space to store a bike in the garage. If you commute to work on a folding bike, you can easily tuck it out of the way when you arrive.

Advantages of folding bikes

One of the major advantages of small-wheeled bikes is that they are usually designed to fold up into a small volume. The advantages of this fall into two categories – portability and storage.

All folding bikes take up much less room when folded than when configured for riding. This makes them convenient to store – and vastly more convenient

A Brompton being carried in folded configuration. The resulting package is incredibly compact – and yet this is still a bike with great capability. (Courtesy Brompton)

Small-wheeled pedal machines – a better way of cycling

A Bike Friday pakiT. It is available with a non-greasy belt drive. If you live in an apartment, a folding bike allows for easy access and convenient storage. (Courtesy Bike Friday)

The second major advantage of a folding bike is that it is much more portable than a conventional large-wheeled bike. This opens enormous possibilities. If you live in a high-rise apartment, you can easily take your bike with you in the lift. (In fact, if you use one of the many covers or carry-bags available, people won't even know that you're carrying a bike.) You can also carry your folded bike into your abode without having to painstakingly manoeuvre the machine through the doorway – and we've all found how

handlebars and pedals of a conventional bikes tend to catch on door jambs!

But it's not only into your home that you can take a folding bike. With a folder, travel with your bike is an immediate option. Pop your bike into the boot of your car and you can take it with you – anywhere. Perhaps you're travelling to a nearby city, and you'd like to go for a ride on the cycle paths around the city centre. Put the bike into the boot, drive to the city, open the boot and unfold your bike and you're set to go. And

Brompton was bought in its place of birth – London, UK – and came home to the other side of the world in a suitcase. Now it was a slightly larger-than-normal suitcase – in part because the bike was well-clad in protective bubble-wrap – but it travelled without any extra charges at all.

When there are public transport travel legs involved, even cycle touring becomes much easier on a folder (more on this in Chapter 6). And talking of pubic transport, in many circumstances (but not all) your folding bike can come with you on public transport. For example, my Brompton has been with me on many trains – but not buses. (Carrying a folder in the passenger compartment of a bus may be pushing it; don't assume access but instead enquire well beforehand. Covering the bike will usually gain better results – it's then just a package, not a bike.)

you don't need to go alone: most folding bikes are small enough that two or even three can be fitted into the luggage space of normal cars.

And that travel can be to distant places. I've flown my Brompton around the country. Packed in a cardboard box, most airport check-in staff don't even believe it's a bike. At the other end, it can go into a cab along with normal luggage. Even at a hotel, no eyebrows will be raised when you take it to your room – and yet whenever you want to, you can unpack the bike and go riding. It is a wonderful way of relaxing on a business trip – going for a ride on your favourite machine in a new place.

International travel with your bike? Again, it's completely possible. My current

A Brompton part way through the fold process. The bike sits stably like this, so it's also a good way to park it. (Courtesy Brompton)

Small-wheeled pedal machines – a better way of cycling

In fact, travel on a train is one of my funniest memories of my folding Brompton. I'd driven interstate on a family visit, and, of course, I'd taken my Brommie with me in the boot of the car. The bike stayed folded in my bedroom for most of the visit, but one day I decided I'd ride a cycle path to a nearby town, and then take the vintage steam train home again. The ride went smoothly, and a little while later I was boarding the steam train, carrying the folded Brompton. I settled down to enjoy the train ride, then noticed out of the corner of my eye that some rather loud tourists on an adjoining seat were eyeing up the machine. I don't think they knew what it was – not just that they didn't know it was a Brompton … I don't think they *even knew it was a bike*. I was getting off at the next stop, so there wasn't much time to say anything.

At the next station I left the train and placed the folded bike on the platform – as it turned out, right opposite the open train window where the tourists sat. Unfolding a Brompton is a magical sight for the uninitiated, and as I extended the seat-post, unfolded the handlebars, locked the front wheel into place and flicked out the rear wheel, a stunned silence fell over the group of tourists. I clicked down the folding pedal and, less than 30 seconds after getting off the train, I was riding off, leaving behind an incredulous, open-mouthed group staring through the window!

A friend of mine takes his folding Dahon with him in his small aircraft, and I've met people who have taken folding bikes with them around the world in sailing yachts. In short, a folding bike can give you immense freedom and fun, in addition to being practical and easily stored in your home.

Disadvantages of folding bikes

Folding bikes also have some disadvantages. The first is that to fold into the smallest volume possible, the

Most folding bikes use long, unsupported seat-posts and handlebar stems. The result of this is that these components are more prone to flex, diminishing pedal energy. (Courtesy Dahon)

frame design has shortcomings in terms of its stiffness. To put this another way, if you were designing a bike to be as stiff and light as possible, and it didn't need to fold, the frame design would be very unlikely to look like any folding bike frame!

The two key areas where this occurs are in the use of long seat-posts, and long handlebar stems. The handlebar stem normally folds close to the frame, and the seat-post slides into the vertical frame tube. The result of these design requirements is that folding bikes tend to be less stiff in these two critical areas – the handlebar stem and seat-post. Note that I am *not* saying that folding bikes will break at those points; instead I am suggesting that there is likely to be some flex with these parts – and typically quite a lot more than a traditional diamond-frame bike. This flex subtracts some of your pedalling energy.

A second disadvantage (that may not be a disadvantage to you) is that folders tend to be very carefully designed – every part is matched so that when the bike is folded, nothing clashes. Therefore, if you – say – change what is usually the fairly hard, compact seat for a large cushy one, you may find that the bike no longer folds correctly, or doesn't fit into its normal carrying box or bag. The same with accessories like new pedals, carriers, lights or mirrors – these need to be carefully selected if they're not to subtract from the folded experience.

When compared to traditional bikes, folding bikes are expensive. Now I can hear you saying that you just looked on-line and what am I talking about? – there are a whole lot of folders that are very cheap! So perhaps I should have said: *high quality folding bikes with a good reputation* are expensive. This is the case for a few reasons. First, the better the folder, usually the more bespoke parts that the manufacturer has used. Making unique parts is much more expensive that buying a part used in all bikes and made in the hundreds of thousands. Second, good quality folding bikes are typically hand-built by craftspeople making relatively few machines.

Bikes like Brompton, Bike Friday and Birdy are all relatively expensive – and they will also take you

Most high-quality folding bikes use many bespoke parts. This makes finding replacements more difficult, and also means that making changes (eg fitting a larger seat or new lighting system) may impact on the folding ease or folded package size. (Courtesy Brompton)

around the world, give many years of good service, and hold their value well. And if you can't afford that calibre of machine? You're still not excluded – Dahon, for example, make good folding bikes that are well-priced, especially secondhand.

Folding bike suspension

As discussed previously, small-wheeled bikes benefit substantially in ride quality from having suspension. However, suspension adds to the cost of producing a bike, and on a folding bike where there is little room and the bike needs to be engineered with the folding capability, suspension adds another layer of complexity and cost.

So does that mean you don't want suspension? No, not at all! But it does mean that typically there will be a trade-off – with suspension, the bike will cost more, or be slower to fold, or be a bigger package when folded. Some of these trade-offs can be minimised if the bike has suspension only at the rear.

Folding bike gearing

Another aspect to carefully consider is gearing.

Firstly, how many gears are available? Many folders use internally geared hubs that provide, for example, three or five ratios. Without a derailleur, the gearing system is reliable and less likely to foul something when the bike is being transported. However, climbing mountains and then sprinting down the other side won't be possible – the range of gearing will be too limited. Other folders are available with derailleur gears, sometimes working in conjunction with an internally geared hub, and so have many ratios.

As covered in Chapter 1, the fact that the bike has small wheels doesn't mean that it will always be low-geared. However, low gearing is just what you may want! If you are buying a bike with a small number of ratios, and you're buying a folder so that you can take it away with you on casual holiday trips where you'll just be pottering along, many folding bikes will have gearing that's too high. After all, you can always roll

A folding bike can be stored almost anywhere. Carry it outside, unfold it, and you're on your way – it's a fabulous feeling of freedom. (Courtesy Bike Friday)

down hills (no pedalling needed), so I think it is better to have gearing too low rather than too high. A folder that you take with you is more likely to meet roads with which you're unfamiliar, and that includes those with grades.

Selecting a folding bike

Picking the correct folding bike is really important. So much of the choice depends on what you are going to do with the bike – how you are going to use it. Much more so than with a traditional bike, picking the wrong folder can mean you end up with a machine that proves to be a waste of money because it cannot do what you want it to do.

For example, let's say that you will primarily be taking the folder with you on holiday. The bike will be folded once, packed carefully, freighted to the destination then unfolded at the other end, being used for day trips for two weeks while on holiday. When the holiday is over, the process will be reversed – the bike folded and then freighted home. In that situation, it doesn't matter much how long the bike takes to fold and unfold, and it doesn't matter if the folded package isn't quite as compact as another design of folder. What *is* important is that the bike is comfortable to ride over unknown roads (so for example, is equipped with suspension) and has plenty of gears. You also want a reliable machine – imagine arriving at your holiday destination, only to have the bike break down!

Contrast that requirement with one where you are using the folding bike for commuting, with public transport (eg a train) making up part of that daily journey. Let's say the route you ride is flat and smooth. In that situation, the bike needs to be quick and easy to fold and unfold (and be reliable doing this hundreds of times a year). It needs to be light, easily carried and be able to take whatever you need to take with you to your workplace – whether that's your lunchbox or briefcase! The bike will also need adequate mudguards (fenders) and lighting, and because of the flat grades, will not need more than two or three gears. Reliability is important, and for this

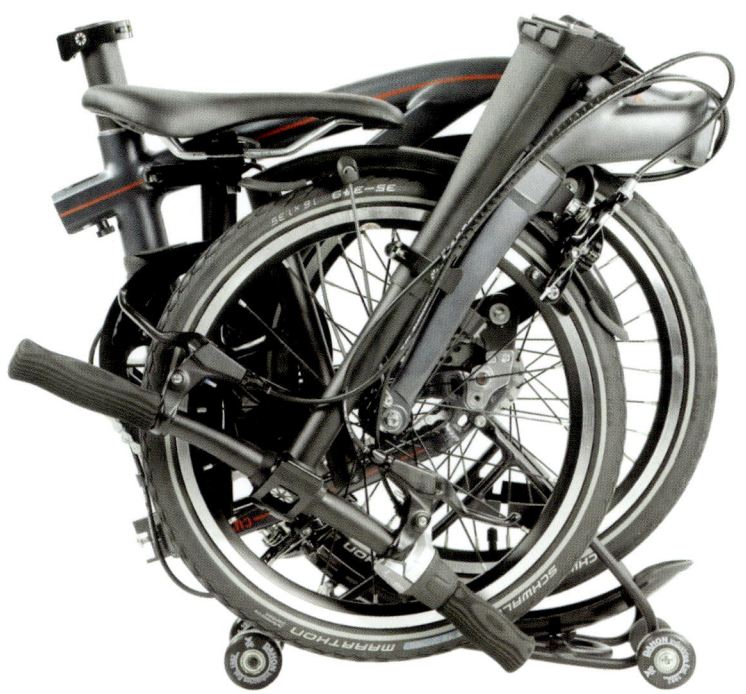

A Dahon Curl. Note the small wheels at the bottom that allow the bike to be rolled along on smooth, flat surfaces. (Courtesy Dahon)

application you can choose a bike with or without suspension.

Finally in these examples, perhaps you want the convenience of being able to easily carry the bike in your car – just for those times when you want to do it. For the most part, the bike will stay in its unfolded orientation – so you want a general-purpose bike that just happens to fold. This type of machine can be much cheaper – if it were to fail, it might be a little inconvenient, but that's all. It can take longer to fold, and form a more unwieldy package when it has been folded. Because you're not going to be on the bike every day, a little more frame flex or a slightly heavier weight will make very little difference. Suspension? In this cost range, the bike probably won't have it.

The selection of the correct folder for your application should always start with *the use you're going to make of the bike*, not aspects such as frame material, wheel size, presence or absence of suspension or the number of gears the bike has. From

Small-wheeled pedal machines – a better way of cycling

A low-cost bike, unfolded and folded. What do you hold when you are carrying it in folded form? More expensive folding bikes have frame designs that allow easy carrying.
(Courtesy Kogan)

the usage you intend to make of the bike, prioritise what is most important. Here's a list to help you get started:

Folded size and shape

The smaller the bike, the easier it will be to take on public transport, and the easier it will be to find a spot for it to be stored. However, the smaller the folded size, typically the smaller the wheels (and so the poorer the ride if suspension is not fitted).

Ease of folding

All folding bikes require familiarity with their folding sequence before you will be anywhere near as fast as achieved by the bike maker in their online videos! So if the video shows the bike taking 30 seconds to fold, immediately double that as a minimum. Those bikes where folding requires tools, or parts to be disassembled, will take longer. Remember, that might not matter much if you are using the bike in an application where folding time isn't important. But in other situations, folding and unfolding time is very important. A slow time can even be dangerous – eg when you alight from a train on a dark remote platform, you want to be on your way quite quickly.

Weight

A heavier bike will take more energy to propel, especially uphill. However, it is when carrying the bike where you really notice a heavier folder. Is the bike too heavy for you to lift into an overhead luggage rack? Can you easily carry the bike 50 metres (yards)? Lightness costs money, and so this is an area where you may have to compromise.

Suspension

As I've indicated elsewhere in this book, I like suspension on small-wheeled pedal machines. However, there are plenty of people who ride a long way, often over poor terrain, who are not worried by the absence of suspension. A lot comes back to how susceptible you are to bumps. If you easily get head- or backaches when riding large-

A Birdy folding bike with front and rear suspension. In practice it is slower to fold than a Brompton, but does have better ride quality and a wider range of gearing. (Courtesy Riese und Müller)

wheel bikes on bumpy roads, ensure that you test ride a folder with and without suspension before buying.

Gears

The number of gears, whether they are internal hub or derailleur, and the overall gearing are all important aspects to consider. Changing the overall gearing, especially if the bike is being custom built for you, or is being bought from a good bike shop, is straightforward.

Variety of frame sizes

Many folders are made in only one frame size, with sufficient adjustment possible for most riders in the handlebar and seat heights. However, if you have any special requirements, or you have a strong preference for a specific riding position, you should consider whether the chosen bike can be configured to suit your needs. Remember that making major

changes of the sort you can on a normal bike (eg changing handlebar reach) may not be possible if the bike is still to properly fold.

Accessories

What accessories are you likely to want – and which are available that will fit the bike? For example, are you likely to want just a small pannier that can be easily detached and taken with you as hand luggage? Or will you want to load up the bike, and so want lots of storage space? Are you going to be riding a lot at night, and will want powerful lights? If so, what lights will fit and still allow the bike to be easily and neatly folded? Do you need an added handle to make carrying the bike easier?

Test riding

Don't buy a folding bike before you have ridden it, folded it, carried it, and unfolded it.

The front pannier on this Brompton is easily unclipped. It also has a handle, so you can carry the folded bike in one hand and the pannier in the other. (Courtesy Brompton)

All folding bikes look a little complex to fold and unfold when you're not used to it, but ensure that you don't just watch someone else do it, but instead actually fold and unfold the bike yourself. Are there any awkward catches to undo, or movements that you find difficult to make? Do the cables and chain fold neatly out of the way, or do they get disorganised or tangled? Are there multiple things that need to be configured before the bike can be folded – for example, the pedals in just the right position, or the gears set to one

specific ratio? (These aren't necessarily negatives, but they're aspects to find out about.)

Can the folded bike actually fit into the space you have available? The best example of this is the boot of your car – some boots appear to magically get smaller when you try to putting a folding bike into them! Others, especially in modern sedans, have high loading lips and small openings, making it more awkward to insert and retrieve a bike.

When the bike is folded, how easy is it to carry? All

folding bikes will be carried at one point or another, and depending on the use you're making of it, you might be carrying it a lot. Is there an easy handgrip by which you can lift and carry the bike? Does the folded bike have wheels that allow you to roll it along on smooth surfaces? If so, how easy is this in practice? Can you carry the bike with both your left and right arms, or is it 'handed'? (Carrying a bike with just one hand will be tiring – you want to be able to swap hands.)

Take the bike for a good test ride – at least 30 minutes. Is the riding position comfortable for you? What is the ride quality like? On a folder that you take with you to new places, you will meet unfamiliar roads that may be bumpier than you're normally on. Do you need suspension, or are you the sort of person who just shrugs off bumps and vibration? If the bike does have suspension, how well does it absorb bumps? Is it effective only on big bumps but lets a lot of vibration through? Does the suspension bounce at your speed of pedalling? (If it does, remember this will absorb a lot of your pedalling energy.)

Is the machine twitchy in its response, and hard to balance? Some folders have, in conventional bike terms, rather odd steering geometry – something you may find disconcerting. Can you ride one-handed and signal with the other?

How hard is it to achieve a good speed? Frame flex and high rolling resistance are often difficult to separately identify – but you'll be able to feel their presence by the high amount of energy that you need to expend to maintain a good speed. If you can find any hills on which to test the bike, great! Up a hill can you stand and pedal with the bike staying stable – or alternatively, can you drop to a really low gear and increase your cadence? Keep in mind that when you're test-riding the bike, you'll likely be carrying nothing – not even a full drink bottle – so in actual use, the pedalling effort will be higher.

Finally, do you feel happy, comfortable and relaxed with the purchase? If you have doubts, test ride a different machine. You can always return to the first one later, if in fact that one proved to be the best.

Chapter 4
Recumbent trikes

So far, we've looked at small-wheeled bicycles – but what about small-wheeled tricycles, and especially those in which you lie back with the pedals located in front of you? These machines are called recumbent trikes.

I am a real fan of small-wheeled recumbent trikes. They are incredibly comfortable, super-stable, a lot of fun to ride, and are also suitable for people with back or balance problems who find it difficult or uncomfortable to ride a bike. Trikes make brilliant

A recumbent trike – two front steering wheels, and one rear-driven wheel. The shaped, semi-reclined seat is like sitting in a lounge chair, and you quickly get used to the forward pedals. Steering is by the two side-mounted handlebars. (Courtesy Greenspeed)

Trikes are huge fun; good quality machines steer with precision, can corner fast (and you can keep on pedalling), and are stable, even in slippery conditions.

long-distance touring machines, and, especially where there are extensive cycle paths, they are excellent commuters.

Recumbent trikes have three wheels, normally with two steering wheels at the front, and one driven wheel at the back. (This is sometimes called a 'tadpole' design.) They are wide and low, with the rider seated on a semi-reclining, soft seat. The pedals are out and ahead of the rider, rather than being below them. Steering is by handlebars, usually located each side of the seat. Most trikes use many gears. Some trikes have suspension, and some can be folded, halving their storage length.

But, as with any form of pedal transport, recumbent trikes have advantages and disadvantages. I'll look at these first and then cover some aspects to consider when selecting a recumbent trike.

Disadvantages

A recumbent trike is a larger vehicle than a bike. More specifically, it is wider and heavier – both in

storage and on the road. If you want to store the trike along one wall of your garage, you'll find it takes up more space than a bike. If you're hugging the narrow shoulder of a road carrying a lot of traffic, you'll take up more width than a bike. If you are riding on a narrow cycle trail and someone comes the other way, you may need to pull off the trail to let them pass.

In terms of storage, you have a few choices. One is to select a folding trike and fold it after each ride. That's quick and easy. (In fact, if you live in a high-rise, you can easily fit a folded trike into the lift and then store it in your abode.) Another choice is to simply find a space for the trike in your garage. Some people even place a little lockable shelter (eg a small, cheap shed) in their garden so that the trike can be tucked into its own home.

Carrying a trike in a car is possible but a bit clumsy. Even trikes that fold are far bulkier than – say – the Brompton cycles covered in the previous chapter. A folding trike can be fitted in the boot (trunk) of many cars, but it is an awkward shape to get in and out. Carrying a trike on public transport isn't something that is easily done.

And what about the width of the trike on the road? In short, if the road is narrow and dangerous for a bike, it will also be narrow and dangerous for a trike. But if there's a cycle lane, or a breakdown lane, or even just not much traffic, the trike will be fine. When passing a trike, car drivers typically give a trike far more room than they do for bikes. Often, the driver will hang back until there's no traffic coming the other way and then pass on the other side of the road. With a

Because of the greater width and lower height of a trike compared with a bike, you need to ensure you can be easily seen. At night use good lighting, and in all conditions use a flag. This was my first recumbent trike.

flag mounted (always use a flag on recumbent cycle machines) and the unusual shape of a trike, drivers are much more likely to see you than if you're on a bike. However, one exception to this is if you're in slow-moving traffic and positioned in a driver's rear three-quarters blind-spot. In that situation, you will be below the level of the car's windows – that's why you should always use a flag. At night, use plenty of lighting.

And then there's weight. Because a trike has three wheels and a more extensive frame, trikes weigh more than bikes. On flat roads that makes little difference (for the technically minded, the extra rolling resistance caused by the additional wheel isn't a lot in absolute terms), but up hills you will have to push a bit harder.

However, this is more than compensated for by the number of gears available, and how slowly you can ride if required – and how fast you'll go down the other side of the hill! That is, compared with a bike, trikes are slower up hills and faster down hills.

Finally, there's the cost. Trikes cost more than bikes – but then again, they also hold their value better, and have a much longer life (a frame guarantee of 10 years and the use of top quality components is common).

Advantages
Trikes are supremely comfortable – I think, the most comfortable machines with pedals ever invented!

Trikes are excellent touring machines. This is the air suspension trike that I designed and built, shown here carrying a full load of touring gear.

Instead of sitting on a narrow seat less than the size of your hand, you're lying back in the equivalent of a reclining armchair. The pressure on your body is spread over a far larger area, and the shape of the seat is superbly supporting. (In fact, I know of some people who sit on their trike when they want to read a book. Who'd go sit on a bike if they wanted to relax?) The pedalling position is natural and comfortable – after a few minutes, you forget that you even have your legs out in front rather than below you.

Trikes are stable. That means you don't have to constantly balance yourself, and it's very difficult indeed to fall over. When you're riding along, and one wheel hits a pebble, or some sand, or some oil,

or a slippery wet white line, or falls off the edge of the path, you just make a steering correction and keep right on riding. On a bike, you'd have possibly been pitched head-first over the handlebars …

Trikes are also excellent load carriers. When you are shopping, you can load the panniers without needing to balance it like a bike, or having to stop it rolling forward and falling off its stand. In comparison with a bike, when being loaded, the trike just sits there. Then, when you pedal off on the trike, there are no wobbles, no 'I-have-to-get-used-to-the-extra-load' feeling of instability that's always the case with a bike.

Trike stability also means there's no minimum riding speed. You can climb a steep hill at literally less than

The Greenspeed Magnum SD in touring form. On loose surfaces, trikes are much more stable than any bike.
(Courtesy Greenspeed)

Trikes are excellent towing machines. They are stable, and, because they are usually fitted with lots of gears, they can tow heavy loads with ease. Because they don't move from side to side when being pedalled, they're also more stable than a bike when towing a child trailer.

a walking pace, pushing along easily in first gear. Or you can pull over and admire a view, take a drink, have a rest, talk to a passer-by – all without taking your feet off the pedals or changing your seating position.

Trikes are fun – and they're simply nothing like a bike to ride. Instead, they're more like a sports car or go-kart – quick steering, low to the ground, fast around corners, nimble and with good grip. Well-designed trikes are surprisingly sophisticated in their steering, with no scrubbing (even in tight corners) and no steering kickback, even when a wheel hits a pebble. If you like the feel of a machine that's 'at one' with the road, you'll love riding a trike. Also, because the pedals are further off the ground than on a bike, you can keep pedalling, even when you're cornering hard. That means if you want to go fast – even if the route is twisty – you can.

Trikes are good at towing. If you want to tow a trailer, you'll find a trike far more stable than a bike. You can park wherever you want without propping up the bike, and the front of the trailer doesn't sway from side to side as it does with a bike. (That makes a child in a child trailer much more comfortable.) In fact, whether you want to tour a country, ride down to the shops for bread and milk, or pull a trailer, a trike is a stable, secure load-carrying platform.

Trike choices

Trikes are available with a variety of wheel sizes, but 16 and 20-inch designs are the most common. (Note also that some trikes use a larger rear wheel than the front wheels.) Trikes with smaller wheels tend to have a firmer ride (unless they have suspension – more on this in a moment), but they are more compact than those with larger wheels.

Trikes are available in folding and non-folding designs. The most compact trike for transport or storage is thus a folding design with 16-inch wheels. So if you want to be able to transport or store your trike easily, consider a small-wheeled folder. On the other hand, if you expect to only ever ride out on day trips from where you live, and you have space to store an unfolded trike, buy one with larger wheels that doesn't fold. For the same quality, it will be a little cheaper, more rigid and ride a little better.

Any trike that you buy should be equipped with a lot of gears. One of my trikes had 81 gears – three front cogs, 9 rear cogs and a three-speed internal rear hub. At the time, I lived in an area with extremely steep hills, and this gear range allowed me to ride at any speed from a very slow walking pace – to travelling at 80km/h (50mph) down hills!

Recumbent bikes?

As you can see from this chapter, I very much like recumbent trikes. They're comfortable, stable, precise in handling, and fun. Not to mention being excellent touring machines, even with big loads. So, do these attributes apply to recumbent *bikes*?

For me, no.

Recumbent bikes have advantages over conventional upright bikes in terms of the size of the seat (and larger certainly equals more comfortable) and lower aerodynamic drag (ie less wind resistance). However, in either long- or short-wheelbase form, I've found them to be less stable than conventional bikes – and of course infinitely less stable than trikes – and to have little or no advantage in load carrying or touring over conventional bikes.

But look – all unconventional pedal machines are worth exploring, and if a recumbent bike is attractive to you, by all means go and test ride one. But I chose to sell my short wheelbase recumbent bike, and disassemble the long-wheelbase recumbent bike that I designed and built. They're not for me!

The other reason that you want lots of gears on a trike is that, unlike a bike, you cannot stand to get greater pedalling force. On a trike, you can of course push back against the seat and so develop very high pedal forces, but this approach tends to cause knee injuries. Instead, it's better on a trike to select a lower gear and maintain your preferred cadence.

Trikes are commonly available with and without suspension. The well-regarded Greenspeed range of trikes, for example, do not use mechanical suspension. Instead they use a mesh seat supported by elastic cording. The seat 'gives' over bumps, and for their more off-road designs, Greenspeed use balloon tyres run at lower pressures. For many people, that combination is fine, although I prefer trikes that use suspension. HP Velotechnik produces trikes with and without suspension, with its 'Scorpion fs' model a well-known suspension design.

When deciding whether to select a trike with suspension, again your choice depends on the sort of roads you will be riding over. A non-suspension trike is likely to be fine for most riders, who traverse good quality concrete or bitumen cycle trails and roads. However, if you intend riding on poorer surfaces (like pebbled dirt, or rough, pot-holey bitumen), then a suspension trike will give a much smoother ride. A suspension trike will also corner better over bumpy surfaces.

Unlike a normal upright bike, the suspension in a trike can be designed so that very little of the rider's energy is lost in the suspension. This is because the rider's leg pushes are forwards, rather than downwards. However, if the chain pull-line isn't set correctly, the rear of the trike can squat with each pedal stroke – and *that* wastes energy! Again, well-designed suspension trikes overcome this with anti-squat rear suspension.

leverage ratios that give both lighter and more stable steering.

Trikes are available with aluminium or steel frames. As with bikes, it's easy to highlight the advantage of one material over the other – however, in fact, there are pluses and minuses of each. Aluminium is lighter than steel – but it also has less strength and so has to be made thicker. However, if it is made thicker only in certain high-stress areas, an overall weight saving can be gained. Aluminium has less fatigue strength than steel – something I found out the hard way when I built my first recumbent trike from aluminium square tube! High quality steel – like chrome moly – is tough and strong. Because thin wall thicknesses can be used, it can also be reasonably light. Chrome moly can be overloaded and then spring back into its original shape, and chrome moly can also be repaired at almost any mechanical workshop in the world that has brazing equipment – important if you are touring to far-flung places.

The stiffness of a trike is in some respects more important than that of a bike, because, unlike a bike, a trike has its 'bottom bracket' (the pedal axle) mounted on an untriangulated boom. This boom tries to flex each time you pedal, and any flexing of this sort takes away some of your pedalling energy – especially when applying high pedal forces up hills. It's a little like when you are riding a bike and pull on the handlebars to get a better pedal push. If the handlebars flex towards you, your pedalling will be diminished in power. In the same way, you don't want a flexing boom on a trike.

Because a trike is a three-wheeled vehicle with steering of two wheels (and all the geometry considerations that results from that), and because the frame design of a trike is more complex than a bike, I recommend that you buy a trike only from a reputable, well-established manufacturer. The cost will be higher (perhaps much higher) than buying a cheap no-name trike, but the quality of the machine in areas like steering, frame stiffness and durability will be much better.

And, if you're even just considering buying a trike,

This older Greenspeed trike uses chrome moly steel for the frame. Current Greenspeeds use aluminium – there are advantages and disadvantages to both materials.

Steering is important in a trike. The cheapest steering systems are designs that use steering arms connected straight to the king-pins (steering swivels). Moving the ends of the steering arms sideways steers the trike. However, this steering motion isn't very natural, as you effectively need to push your hands sideways – not your direction of natural strength. The very direct ratio can also make the steering twitchy. Much better are steering systems that use a system with fore-aft movement of the steering handlebars, with the handlebars connected to the steering swivels by links. In addition to making use of your greater arm strength that's achievable in this direction, the steering linkages can incorporate

Small-wheeled pedal machines – a better way of cycling

go and ride one! I discovered trikes quite serendipitously. I was on a business trip and I noticed a factory that had a sign showing a weird (to my eyes), recumbent three-wheeler with pedals out the front. Having some time to spare, and intrigued by the picture, I went in and asked what they built. They showed me a recumbent trike, and suggested I take one for a ride. Off I went, pedalling around the industrial area on a machine that went, steered and rode like nothing I'd ever been on. When I returned, a big smile was splitting my face – and the factory staff smiled back. "That's the trike grin!" they said. The factory was the one that produced Greenspeed trikes, and I subsequently bought one – and then built three recumbent trikes of my own design.

Because you don't have to unclip from pedals, a trike is a wonderful machine on which to stop and admire the view. It's also comfortable to sit like this (perhaps with pedals unclipped) for half an hour.

Trikes that fold are available, like this Greenspeed GT20. However, they are still much bulkier than a small-wheeled folding bike.
(Courtesy Greenspeed)

Chapter 5

Commuting

Commuting involves a daily ride to a place of work, study or leisure. The requirements of commuting are different from other forms of cycling – primarily in the fact that much commuting is non-discretional. That is, you don't have a choice as to your destination, or often the time you need to be there.

In my cycling life, I have regularly commuted only once – and I did it all wrongly! I was studying at university as a 17-year-old, and decided to ride my bike to the campus each day. The round trip was 16km (10mi). So what were the problems?

The first problem was I wasn't fit enough. This surprised me, because at the time I often went for rides much longer than this. But in commuting I was doing the ride *every day* – not just occasionally.

The next problem was that I did the ride in all weathers. It's a long time ago now, but I remember one day when it was raining all the way. Visibility was terrible, I was on a main road with plenty of traffic, I kept getting splashed with water, and my bike lights broke down. It was just awful!

The third problem was the bike I was riding – a low-cost, low-quality machine that was heavy and not particularly well balanced.

So where does that leave us? Cycle commuting is

Commuting on a Brompton. The front bag is large enough to carry items like lunch and a laptop. (Courtesy Brompton)

likely to work best if you choose to cycle *only some of the time*. If you live in a country with cold winters, cycle only in summer. If you live in a country with very hot summers, ride only in the milder seasons. In other words, have an alternative form of transport that you can take whenever you don't wish to cycle. This also takes into account the real-world circumstances of running late, or recovering after the night before, or a family crisis like a sick child.

You also need to be fitter than the bare travel distance suggests. After all, you cannot arrive exhausted from your ride – your work colleagues will soon get sick of that! Having available another form of transport to use instead of cycling helps in this regard too – you can gradually build up the number of days you cycle.

Finally, while I have read some suggestions that short commuting can be done on any old bike you happen to have, I think for any commuting you need a high-quality machine that is well-equipped, stable and comfortable.

Small wheels allow plenty of space above the wheels for carrying goods on a commute. This Brompton is fitted with its sturdy optional carrier – the bike still folds up to a tiny bundle with the carrier in place.

Fixed or folding?

Selecting a folding small-wheel bike has plenty of advantages for commuters. If the bike is compact and quick to fold and unfold, it's likely that you will be able to use public transport (eg a train or tram) as part of your commute. That allows your commute to be longer than would be comfortable by bicycle alone.

Using a folding cycle also gives you greater flexibility. For example, perhaps on a Friday evening you and your partner agree to have dinner near where you work. He or she will drive in, you'll meet and have dinner, and then the bike can be easily folded and brought home in the car.

A folding bicycle also makes the machine easier to store at your workplace – eg, it could be taken up in a lift and placed near where you work. That also means you can keep an eye on it – perhaps rather than worrying if your pride and joy is currently being stolen from a public rack!

A fixed small-wheel commuter won't have those advantages, but all else being equal, it will probably have a stiffer frame and so be a better machine over a longer distance. Both types of bike will have the normal advantages of small-wheeled bikes – a standout being the ability to carry plenty of goods above the front and rear wheels.

Planning your commute

Planning your commute is important – you will need to decide on the best route, and what you will take with you.

If you have been driving or taking public transport to work, you probably have *not* been using the best route for cycling. A freeway or main road with high-speed traffic is probably your fastest way to work, but it will make for a rather unpleasant commute on a bike. It's good, therefore, to explore the different route options, preferably on a weekend – realising of course that on a week day there will likely be a great deal more traffic.

Are there cycle trails or back roads you can use? What routes do other people take who are doing a similar commute? Remember, most people who are cycle commuting aren't doing it because they want to get to work in the fastest way possible; they're doing it because they want to better enjoy the world. As one cycle commuter said to me, "When you are cycle commuting, wind and weather really matter, and you can observe the level of streams and the blossoming of the flowers – and reconnect with the environment." But riding down the narrow shoulder of a road streaming with heavy goods vehicles belching diesel fumes won't achieve this – better to wind your way through quiet back streets.

The next planning step is to decide what you will take with you. This can be divided into two categories – items that will be used at the workplace, and items that you are taking with you because you are riding a bike. I can't think of any jobs (other than working in a cycling shop?) where the clothes that you wear on your bike will also be suitable for the working environment, so you will need different 'work' clothes.

You can achieve this in a few different ways. You can take your work clothes with you each day – but, especially in an office job, how do you keep them presentable? If you roll the clothes (rather than folding them) and shake them out when you arrive, you may be able to keep the clothes uncreased. Another approach is to take the next day's clothes each day and leave the clothes on a hanger overnight. You can even iron your clothes at work, but the practicalities of doing this can become difficult. Perhaps the best approach is to commute by public transport or car once a week and each time bring a week's worth of clothes.

If you ride in warm conditions, you will need to have a shower at your destination. Some modern workplaces have these facilities, however a significant number do not. If no shower facilities exist, are there any nearby local gyms, indoor pools or similar where you might be able to negotiate a daily shower? If not, perhaps a hand basin, soap, a face-washer, a small towel and deodorant might be enough. To state the obvious, you don't want to get a reputation as the smelly co-worker!

If your commuting destination has no facilities

Recumbent trikes

Recumbent trikes (covered in more detail in Chapter 4) are particularly suited to commuting, especially if most of the trip is on cycle paths, and there is room to store the trike at your workplace. The main advantage of the trike is its stability – remember, if you're commuting, the weather conditions will not always be ideal. So if it rains or snows during the day, and the road surface is slippery, your trip home will be much more stable and safe if you have three wheels on the ground, rather than two.

for cyclists, perhaps draw the appropriate people's attention to some of the points in the 'bicycle friendly workplaces' panel shown on the next page.

Do you prepare your lunch at home and then take it to work each day? Do you need to take your laptop computer with you? Each of these is of course easy – but it needs planning. In hot weather you don't want your chicken-salad sandwich breeding bacteria on the way in (so it will need to be kept cool), and the laptop will need to be protected. Imagine if the bike fell over and the laptop shattered … On some small-wheeled bikes (eg a Brompton) a removable front bag will easily store items like a laptop or tablet computer, and lunch.

Unless it is very small and light, I would not suggest wearing a backpack. While a backpack is convenient to carry, it also upsets your balance on the bike – better to have the bike supporting the goods you are carrying, rather than your body.

If you are riding with plenty of other traffic around you, fit a rear vision mirror to either your helmet or cycle. If the bike folds, you may need to select a bike-mounted mirror quite carefully if the mirror isn't to cause clearance problems on the folded bike.

One early decision to make is what you will do if you have a breakdown – including a flat tyre. Plenty of commuters take tools and spare tubes or patches and are quite prepared (and able) to repair a flat tyre by the side of the road or path. However, to be honest, that's not something I'd countenance doing on a

Bicycle-friendly workplaces

Encouraging your employees to ride to work can reap benefits. Employees who are fit and healthy have a higher level of job satisfaction, perform better at work and have better health. Cycling to work saves on car parking spaces and fuel.

Providing end-of-trip facilities is the main thing employers can do to encourage employees to cycle.

Although many employers might not be able to provide all of the following, they could:

○ negotiate access to nearby facilities in gyms or clubs. This could include negotiating non-peak rates or concessional membership if available

○ provide facilities in cooperation with other nearby businesses

○ reimburse employees who incur costs such as gym fees, bike storage fees or bicycle maintenance

Other initiatives to encourage cycling are:

○ allowances such as mileage to employees using bicycles for work purposes

○ salary packaging that could include cost of bikes, accessories, clothing or membership of a club where the employee showers

○ a special deal with a bike shop for discounts

○ membership of cycling organisations that provide access to insurance cover and other support to people who cycle

○ a 'buddy' system to encourage inexperienced cyclists

○ a work bike pool to encourage use of bikes for work purposes

○ a tool library for employees maintaining their own bikes

○ a flexible hours scheme so employees can avoid cycling in peak traffic

The exact needs of employees can vary according to the type of business and the location of the workplace. Employers could encourage a workplace bicycle user group, which can provide feedback on the needs of employees who ride.

(Courtesy Queensland Government Department of Main Roads)

commute – especially for the rear wheel, where you may need to handle a greasy chain. An alternative is to take a can of latex tyre inflater that will seal small punctures and also inflate the flat tyre. Or you can use tyres that are highly puncture resistant, or tubes that are already part-filled with a puncture sealing compound. In all cases, a pump should be part of your equipment.

Even if you're not repairing flat tyres, it makes sense to take along a small tool kit – eg hex keys in sizes that fit the majority of your bike's fasteners, Philips and flat screwdrivers, and a small adjustable spanner. These will be useful if a problem occurs that is simple and quick to fix – for example, the bell becomes loose, or a mudguard (fender) stay needs to be tightened.

Bike equipment

Your commute will be safer, and more comfortable and enjoyable, if you are riding a well-equipped bike.

Commuting bikes should be equipped with effective mudguards (fenders) to prevent water on the road from spraying onto you. The mudguards should *more than* cover the width of the tyres, and also cover a satisfactory amount of the wheels' circumferences. Flexible rubber flap extensions at the rear edges of mudguards can prevent odd splashes from reaching you. If you're unsure of how effective the mudguards on a new bike are, test them by riding through puddles!

Commuting cycles need good lighting and reflectors. Lights – front, back and side – should be visible from a long distance and at a wide variety of viewing angles. The front and rear lights shouldn't use overly narrow beams (or they will not be visible from an angle) and the rear light should be designed so it has some sideways output. (If it doesn't, you can add extra lights that achieve this.)

Organise your lighting so that you won't unexpectedly be left with dull or non-working lights. If you are using rechargeable lights, develop a routine for charging – every Sunday evening, for example. If you use lights with non-rechargeable batteries, replace them frequently (eg every month) and carry

This large, expandable bag is perfect for carrying 'work' clothes, lunch and a small tool kit.
(Courtesy Moulton Bicycle Company)

spares. Lights powered by a dynamo – especially a hub dynamo – are the most reliable, although not the brightest.

Reflectors are very effective, especially on roads where you are mixing with cars. Front, rear and side reflectors should be fitted, and if they move (eg they're mounted on wheels or pedals), they're even more effective.

If you are commuting on quiet cycle paths that run through parks, fit adequate forward lighting so that you will be able to see small animals from a good distance. Hitting even a squirrel can knock you from your bike. If you place an additional narrow-beam light on your helmet, you can quickly turn your head to aim it at odd noises and rustles. Such a light is also useful for ensuring specific car drivers have seen you, eg at intersections.

Bright clothing is a must, and clothing that integrates reflective material is best of all. Note that if you're on a tight budget, 'high visibility' clothing sold for outdoor workers can be much cheaper than bespoke cycling gear. If your commute is a longer one, use clothing that can be added or removed in layers.

A good quality helmet is vital. Ensure it fits well (so for example, you don't have a weird hair style after you take it off!), is comfortable, and has plenty of airflow. Make sure that no matter how you move your head, the helmet cannot fall off.

A mobile phone (cell phone) mounted on the handlebars will allow you to check the time, monitor a map or show you speed and distance. However, don't be tempted to listen to music – you want to be able to hear what is happening around you.

Especially in hot climates, take plenty of easily-accessible water. That might involve a hydration bladder or frame-mount bottles.

Finally, have a means of locking your bike. Even if you have secure bike accommodation at your destination, taking any detours on the way home (eg to shops) will need a lock.

When things go wrong

So what could go wrong on a cycle commute, then? Try this list from cycle commuter Stephen Nurse: missing a train, destroying clothes when they rub on a bike wheel, draining of the water bottle on the train floor, accidentally dropping the helmet on the train tracks, breaking a gear cable, bike breaking and

A compact multi-purpose tool is good insurance on your commute. Even if you don't intend to undertake major repairs, it will let you tighten loose fasteners and undertake similar quick and easy jobs.

Small-wheeled pedal machines – a better way of cycling

everyday adventures that help keep cyclists sane and resilient!" he says.

In addition to the equipment mentioned so far, carry a small first aid kit and ensure that you have something that identifies you and gives first-response contacts. If you have specific medical conditions, these should be indicated as well. An engraved wrist band is a good way of communicating this information.

Also, from the very start of your commuting, put aside the money for a cab fare. That way, if you do miss that train or break down, you'll feel no guilt in whistling-up a ride.

And remember, especially if you've thoroughly planned your route and you're well-equipped, nothing may ever go wrong. After all, one recent study showed that commuting cyclists in a major city were twice as happy as other commuters!

having to proceed by cab, a puncture, getting rained on, riding through a thunderstorm and flood, catching the wrong train, running over a dog turd, and spilling casserole in the back of the panniers.

But was he daunted? No, "These are the small

Very bright lighting on a recumbent trike. Note the two rear lights and two side-facing lights. The headlight provides an excellent, relatively wide beam that still has good reach. Reflective tape has been added to the rear mudguard (fender) and parts of the frame. The car in the picture is about 35 metres (yards) away.

Chapter 6

Touring

Cycle touring can range from being fully self-supported – that is, carrying sleeping, cooking, food and water supplies – through to having just one change of clothes, a healthy credit card, and a touring approach that uses plenty of public transport. Both styles of bike touring – and everything in between – can be a lot of fun, so let's take a look at cycle touring on a small-wheeled machine.

Bike travel/packing logistics

Most people who go cycle touring don't start off from where they live – instead, they first travel to a distant location and start from there. For example, they might fly their bike and gear to another country, or pile all the gear into a car and then drive to an interesting location, before touring by bike.

In these situations, using a small-wheeled bicycle can be a major advantage. A folding or separable bike can normally be packed and freighted with little effort. For example, the bike can often be placed inside a suitcase indistinguishable from that being taken by other airline passengers. Suddenly the whole hassle of 'taking a bike' – what with its usual special 'large freight' requirements, surcharges and other problems are gone. Just like that.

However, you won't be freighting a bare bike – instead, you'll want to pack it. That packing might be in cardboard, a suitcase, or some other container.

But what happens to that packaging at the other end? When you get on your bike and ride off into the glorious unknown, what do you do with it?

Bike Friday has an elegant solution in that the bike packing case turns into the trailer, but if you don't take that route, you'll need to consider other options. One is to simply discard the packaging, and then buy new materials when it's time to ship the bike home. For example, bubble-wrap, cardboard and adhesive tape are widely enough available, and sufficiently cheap, that if you were touring for more than (say) a week, it would be worth putting the original packaging in a recycling bin and then buying new for the freight home. That sounds wasteful – but the alternative is to cart the bulky materials with you.

Another solution is to buy a soft bike bag that compresses into a small package for the cycle touring leg. Especially if you are towing a trailer and have a bit more room, this can work well. However, I always remember when we'd just bought two expensive soft bags to protect our (near-new) Bromptons. Along with a Burley Solo child trailer and Burley Nomad cargo carrier, we'd freighted the lot by train to a distant location. Eagerly waiting in the freight arrival area for the delivery of our stuff, we were appalled when we sighted the freight attendant dragging the two bike bags toward us across the rough concrete. Of course, by the time they got to us, holes had been abraded

Left: Moulton APB disassembled and packed in a suitcase. The assembly has been temporarily held together with zip ties to allow it to be easily lifted out in case of airport inspection. Right: The Moulton reassembled and on tour. All the luggage is fully suspended. (Both photos courtesy Jurien Dekter)

in both bags – although luckily the bikes were unharmed. My wife Georgina and I turned to each other and said simultaneously: "Should have packed them in cardboard and bubble-wrap!" – and we've not used soft bags since.

How self-supporting?

Another major decision to make is how, precisely, self-supporting are you going to be? I've not done it, but you could go cycle touring on the basis that you will ride on only nice days, and take public transport on other days. Staying in hotels or other accommodation, and with a mobile phone (and that credit card) you could call up a cab whenever that was a better option – and with a compact folding bike and a single pannier, transport would be no drama. Even with two of you.

On the other hand, and especially in really hot or cold environments, to be self-supporting requires both major endurance and a lot of supplies. I've travelled mostly in hot environments, and there the requirement to take enough water starts to weigh (literally) on your equipment. In a hot environment, you may need 15 litres (4 US gallons) of water a day – that's 15kg (33lb) on its own. And then you'll always need a safety margin, so it's more likely to be a water weight of 20kg

(44lb) – *per day*. (And even on a full touring machine like a recumbent trike, 20kg is a lot to have on top of your other luggage.)

Of course, there's a multitude of variations between 'credit card and a toothbrush' and 'fully self-supporting through the desert.'

If you're new to cycle touring, I suggest that you start off as conservatively as possible. Plan just one night away at a location that is accessible by an easy ride, or by a combination of public transport and a short ride. Especially if you are taking children (or a partner who has previously not cycle toured) it's possible for small issues to become big ones – and the result may be that no-one enjoys the tour! If you live in a climate that has a mild season, go then – less need for water (hot climate) and less need for warm clothing and bedding (cold climate). It may seem rather timid, but putting a toe in the water will show you what works, and what does not.

One of our first Brompton cycle tours involved taking a train and then riding on a purpose-built cycle trail through the countryside. It was pleasant and achievable for a couple and a small child – but it also showed us that our sleeping gear was inadequate for even the mildest of frosts, and that perhaps it might have been better to start off closer to home.

We also took way too much – I will forever remember the shemozzle of the night before departure, where I was riveting together bags that were bursting apart because of the number of bananas we were stuffing in them. (Why bananas? No idea!)

Carrying equipment

Any form of cycle touring requires that your bike is in good mechanical condition and is suitably equipped. Bearings, chain, gears and brakes all need to be in good condition. Your bike will need to have mudguards (fenders) and lights.

You will also want to be really comfortable on the bike, in terms of seat, riding position and handgrips. Any discomfort or mechanical shortcoming of the bike will be magnified if you're tired after spending hours riding, especially over unfamiliar terrain. You don't want to be trying out a brand-new machine by immediately embarking on a tour – instead, sort-out all the little quibbles on rides closer to home.

One of the most important equipment decisions is to work out how you are going to carry equipment on the bike. Especially on a folding machine, you need to ensure that front and rear carriers, bag-mounting blocks, drink bottle mounts, rear vision mirrors, cell phone mounts, and the like, do not inhibit the bike's ability to fold. (It's only when you're adding non-standard accessories that you realise how carefully designed most folding bikes are.)

Positioning heavy gear as close to the centre of the

A good 'toe in the water' with cycle touring is to travel to a location by car and set up camp, going on extended day trips by bike. Here, two Bromptons and a child trailer are being used.

Fabulous scenery and numerous places to camp. Note the brightly-coloured clothing, panniers and trailer.

bike, and as low as possible, will give the least impact on bike handling. For example, here's something you *don't* want to do – place a heavy load behind the rear wheel axle. Why? Because this will reduce the weight on the front wheel, allowing it to skid more easily. Another poor approach is to place weight in widely-mounted panniers – this will make the bike less balanced. You obviously cannot have all the additional load at the centre of the bike frame (that's where you are!), but remember that the further away

from the centre the heavier loads are positioned, the worse the bike handling will be.

Be careful of adding other than very lightweight gear to the handlebars – that is, weight that turns with the steering. This weight adds inertia to the steering and will remove some of the quick response and nimbleness that a small-wheeled bike naturally has.

I suggest that, where they can be accommodated by the bike designs, low-mounted front and rear panniers are fitted, positioned as close to the wheels

Full touring gear for two adults and a child – two Brompton folding cycles, a Burley Solo child trailer, a Burley Nomad cargo trailer, tents, sleeping gear, clothing and emergency supplies. Here, the gear is between trains on its way to the touring location.

The same gear seen while on tour. Note the reflectors, flags and rain covers.

as possible. Heavy items (eg tools and water) can be mounted as far forward as possible on a rear carrier, and lighter weight items (eg clothing) on a front carrier or bag supported by the headstem.

A trailer is an option. A trailer adds rolling resistance and aerodynamic drag, but it moves heavy and/or bulky loads off the bike. Trailers are available in single-wheel and dual-wheel versions, and good quality trailers are also available to transport a child safely. If you have a bike with rear suspension, it is best if

Small-wheeled pedal machines – a better way of cycling

the trailer connects not to the rear wheel axle, but to the suspended bicycle frame.

Most trailers fold, but they're still normally quite large packages, even when folded. So taking a trailer to a distant location adds another sizeable package to the freight logistics – but you may well be glad you went to that extra trouble when you're actually on the tour.

Whatever the approach you decide to take, it is vital that you fully load the bike with all that you intend taking – *and then do extensive trial rides before you embark on your tour.* That is, pack everything – including water and food – and then ride your normal near-home routes carrying the full

Lunch stop. This cycle trail is along the path of an old railway line – rail-trails are excellent for short cycle touring. They're quiet, have gentle grades and are usually well supported by shops and accommodation (if required) en-route.

load. Doing this means that you will often find shortcomings.

Is the bike gearing now too high? Is the handling of the bike now a bit scary going fast downhill? Do your heels clip panniers, or are you prevented turning the handlebars sufficiently far because something gets in the way? Are your lights or reflectors blocked by the extra gear? Are you simply taking way too much, and you need to revisit your whole strategy? Are you fine, but the person you are riding with is clearly overloaded? Is unloading the bike and folding (or disassembling) it now a one hour job – and you've left nowhere near enough time to do that between transport legs?

Whatever, you do, don't leave packing until the night before departure – test your loads thoroughly, well before you leave.

Touring with a 5-year-old. He is riding a tag-along that is also supporting large panniers. Behind this combination is a Burley Nomad cargo trailer. The bike is a Brompton.

The combination seen from the side – we called it 'the road-train.' When I needed a rest, the trailer was swapped to my wife's bike.

What to take

So what gear do you take with you? The following provides a detailed checklist, in part based on one developed by cycle tourer Jim Dirlam.

Bicycle accessories (mounted to bike)
- Front/rear rack and panniers (and/or a trailer)
- Handlebar bag (and mounting bracket)
- Rain covers and/or plastic bags (for non-waterproof panniers)
- Rack bag or PVC dry bag (for rainy tours)
- Seat/frame bag (good for storing tyre repair kit)
- Comfortable saddle
- Water bottles and cages and/or hydration pack
- LCD cycle computer (with new or extra battery)
- LED flashing tail light
- LED head light (or use camping headlamp)
- Mirror (mounted on handlebar or helmet)
- Bell
- Front and rear mudguards (fenders)
- Bungee cords or webbing straps (2-3)
- Bike lock
- Reflectors

Camping gear (in various stuff sacks)
- Tent (1-2 person) plus ground sheet
- Sleeping mat
- Sleeping bag rated for the lowest expected temperatures, plus compression sack
- Sleeping bag liner (for mild/cold camping or hostel use)
- Air pillow (or use clothes in stuff sack)
- Nylon stuff sacks (various sizes, for clothes and gear)
- Self-contained stove with cooking pans
- Fuel bottle (must be specifically designed for carrying fuel)
- Utensils: spork/spoon, fork and knife set (Lexan or titanium)
- Plate and bowl (light weight)

- Small wash-up kit with scourer, dish cloth and detergent
- Insulated travel mug
- Water filter or purifier (for backcountry or international travel)
- Light backpack or daypack (if doing side hikes)
- Clothes pegs (6-8)
- Mosquito/fly head net

Cycling clothes (quantities depend on duration and weather)

- Helmet (proper size and fit) and optional visor
- Cycling jersey or synthetic T-shirt (2-3)
- Cycling shorts (1-2 – maybe 3 for long tours)
- Underwear (3-4 sets)
- Cycling gloves
- Cycling socks (synthetic/wool – 2-3 pairs)
- Clip-in cycling shoes (or trail/running shoes if using toe-clips)

Foul-weather cycling clothes (in nylon stuff sack)

- Long-sleeve jersey/light-mid synthetic/wool zip shirt (1)
- Cycling long-tights/insulated wind pants (1)
- Rain jacket and pants (1 set — waterproof nylon/Gore-Tex)
- Fall/winter gloves/mittens and liners (1 pair)
- Synthetic helmet liner/sweat bands/bandana (1)
- Wool hat (1)
- Arm and leg warmers (1 pair of each)
- Waterproof rain booties/gaiters (1 pair)
- Helmet cover (1)

Camp and town clothes (in nylon stuff sack)

- Presentable clothing suitable for wearing in layers
- Normal shoes (if using cleated cycling shoes)

Documents (in wallet/travel pouch/handlebar bag)

- Driver's licence (or other official photo ID)
- Passport (if travelling internationally)
- ATM/debit card
- Credit card(s) (with bank's hotline number to call if lost/stolen)

- Cash
- Travel tickets
- Photocopies (passport/license, stored in separate place)
- Emergency contact info

Personal Items (usually wearing and/or in handlebar bag)

- Watch
- Sunglasses
- Contact lenses/eyeglasses
- Sunscreen
- Insect repellent
- Lip balm

Gadgets and travel Items (in handlebar bag)

- Cell phone and charger
- LED headlamp and batteries
- Digital camera, memory cards, charger, case
- Laptop or tablet computer
- Maps
- Guidebook
- Pen (2)
- Small notebook
- Reading book
- Small padlock (for hostel lockers – if using)

Bike tools and spare parts (in pouch or zip-lock)

- Pump (pack in bag instead of on bike frame)
- Patch kit and tyre levers
- Spare tubes (1-2)
- Spare tyre
- Degreaser
- Chain lube
- Spokes (3-6)
- QR axle
- Brake/shift cable
- Nuts and bolts and bailing wire (specifically for racks, brakes, etc)
- Handy wipes
- Bicycle multi-tool

Additional repair Items (in pouch or zip-lock)

- Multi-tool/pocket knife

Small-wheeled pedal machines – a better way of cycling

- Duct tape and electrical tape
- Plastic zip ties
- Batteries
- Plastic bags – zip-lock
- Safety pins (4-5 large)
- Parachute cord (5 metres)
- Rubber bands (4-5 heavy-duty)
- Seam sealer (small tube)

Toiletries (in travel pouch or zip-lock)

- Travel towel
- Washcloth
- Soap/shampoo
- Deodorant (travel size)
- Toothbrush and toothpaste
- Toilet paper (small roll in zip-lock)
- Hand sanitiser
- Skin cream
- Nail clippers
- Tweezers
- Hair brush/comb
- Hair ties (for long hair)
- Disposable razor (and shaving cream)
- Women's hygiene products
- Ear plugs
- Prescription medications
- Multi-vitamins

First-aid/other toiletries (in pouch or zip-lock)

- Band-aids (assorted sizes and shapes)
- Antiseptic cream
- Adhesive tape
- Alcohol wipes
- Cotton swabs
- Compress/non-stick gauze pads (med/large size)
- Pain killer tablets
- Anti-chafing cream
- Anti-itch cream
- Muscle relief cream
- Anti-diarrhoea tablets
- Antihistamine tablets
- Elastic bandage
- Snake bite bandage

- Neoprene knee/ankle wrap
- Antibiotics
- Sterile water in sealed plastic vials
- Hydrolyte sachets
- Mild laxatives

Survival items (in pouch or zip-lock)

- Lighter/storm matches and cotton wool kindling
- Compass
- Mirror or polished stainless-steel reflector
- Whistle
- Emergency space blanket
- EPIRB (if out of cell-phone range)
- Dehydrated food (two complete meals)

It's important to understand when looking at this list that you are unlikely to take *all* these items! However, many of these items are small, light and cheap. A good example is a mosquito/fly head net – very easy to pack, and such a benefit in the right conditions.

Setting up for the night, just off the trail. Buy good quality, brand-name tents, sleeping mats and cooking equipment. If you cannot afford new, buy these items secondhand.

When putting together your touring gear, there are some areas you can save money – for example, by assembling your own first aid kit rather than buying one already made-up – but there are other areas where buying cheaply is false economy. Items like your tent, sleeping bag (and sleeping mat) and cooking equipment need to be of high quality if they are to be light and effective. This is one area where 'brand name' items really do outperform much cheaper no-names. If you cannot afford new, buy these quality items secondhand.

Touring Kangaroo Island

Jurien and Connie Dekter cycle-toured Kangaroo Island, off South Australia.

Kangaroo Island is about 145km (90mi) in length and varies from 1-54km (0.5-34mi) in width. Many of the roads are unsealed, with marble-like gravel a common surface. The island has a small population of about 5000 people and a few towns. Land use is primarily farming, but there are also some large nature parks. The coastline is stunning. Access to the island is from the Australian mainland via ferry, a short trip.

Their tour took 10 days and was completed in the middle of summer. It is a good example of an achievable cycle tour, with support nearby in case of a breakdown and accommodation available in some areas if the weather turns poor. Jurien rode a Birdy and Connie a Reach – both small-wheel folding cycles with front and rear suspension.

The partly-loaded bikes on the ferry. In addition to passengers, the ferry carries vehicles of all sizes and shapes.

The catamaran ferry approaching the mainland across the evocatively named Backstairs Passage. Kangaroo Island is in the background.

Arriving at Penneshaw, a tiny town on the island. From here the cycling adventure begins!

After staying overnight in the youth hostel at Penneshaw, Connie tucks into breakfast: energy for what will be a long day – 90km (56mi) from Penneshaw to Flour Cask Bay.

The bikes loaded, a last glimpse of the Penneshaw marina. Jurien is wearing an almost-empty backpack; he hung it over the handlebars soon after this photo was taken.

The view stretches far into the distance. Cycle gloves reduce vibration and soreness, especially on rough surfaces.

Climbing the steep hill out of Penneshaw, standing all the way and in bottom gear. Always remember that when touring, you will likely need lower gearing than you normally use.

Onto the gravel road. Note the numerous, symmetrical corrugations. On surfaces like this, a suspension bike makes riding much more comfortable.

In some places the roads had a good hard-packed dirt surface, but other roads were badly pockmarked – worse than corrugations.

A very dangerous black tiger snake crossing the road. In countries like Australia, your first-aid kit should always include a snakebite treatment bandage. Wherever you are touring, research the local wildlife before you leave home!

This stunning view is very characteristic of Kangaroo Island coastal scenes – steep cliffs bisected by sandy beaches.

This is why you need to pack those seemingly inconsequential things like fly nets! Note the long sleeves for sun protection.

The campsite at Flour Cask Bay. Here there were no people for miles: you need adequate supplies if you are going to camp at sites like these. The next leg is from Flour Cask Bay to Vivonne Bay (75km, 47mi).

After breaking camp at Vivonne Bay, a visit to Little Sahara to view the sand dunes. Ensure you make time when touring to enjoy the sights you're passing.

Layering of clothes allows you to easily match your clothing to the conditions, divesting yourself of layers as the day warms up.

The Flinders Chase National Park covers the western end of the island.

Back on the sealed road. When riding internationally, always memorise the side of the road on which you're supposed to be riding. Stretches of road like these don't normally cause difficulties, but turning at intersections can be problematic unless you concentrate.

More formal camping accommodation like this allows you to shower away the sweat of the day, and make use of facilities like a BBQ and tent sites. Jurien and Connie stayed here for a rest day – although since they explored some of the Flinders Chase National Park (riding 53km/33mi), it wasn't 'rest' as perhaps others know it!

Extraordinary granite rock formations within the park. Note the size of the people at right. The next leg was from Western Kangaroo Island Caravan Park to Stokes Bay (78km/48mi).

Vehicle rollovers are common on Kangaroo Island – the combination of drivers' inexperience on loose surface roads and the treacherous marble-like gravel that many roads are covered in. Most of these accidents occur at relatively slow speeds, so serious injuries are not common.

Stunning beach at Stokes Bay. The waters are clear and unpolluted, and the crowds nowhere to be seen. After a rest day at Stokes Bay, the next leg was to Kingscote (56km, 35mi). Kingscote is the island's largest town – no camping was needed!

Time for a portrait of Connie's Pacific Cycles Reach. The bike carried about 10kg (22lb) of luggage, while Jurien's Birdy was carrying about 20kg (44lb) – mostly camping gear.

Catching-up with some other cycling tourists. This couple was from Germany.

From Kingscote to American River was a 56km (35mi) leg.

The tranquility of American River at dawn. The final leg – American River back to Penneshaw (45km/28mi) – awaits.

Another beautiful Kangaroo Island beach, this one near Prospect Hill.

Connie labouring up a very steep climb between Brown Beach and Penneshaw. Penneshaw is where the mainland ferry docks, so we're back to our starting point. Next to the ferry – and then home.

Chapter 7
Restoration and rebuilding

Old small-wheel pedal machines are special. They represent cycling that's different to the vast majority of bikes, and they're interesting indicators of different social times as well as mechanical design history. So when you stumble across an old small-wheeled bike, especially one of the really historic machines, it's very tempting to grab it with the intention of doing a full restoration.

But stop!

The first question is: do you have the money to spend on the project? In round figures, if you're paying a normal price for a bike in 'needing restoration' condition, by the time you've finished, expect to spend 10-20 times the

initial purchase price. Really? That much? It sounds ludicrous, but if you want to do a really good job, yes, it will cost that much.

See those slightly rusty rims, the chrome flaking off? I'll *restore* them, you say. So the wheels will need to be disassembled, the rims stripped, sanded and polished to perfection before being professionally re-chromed.

When you see a classic bike like this going cheaply, it's easy to get excited, thinking about a full restoration. But always keep in mind that a bike like this will need every single part restored or rebuilt: a process that, if done well, is likely to cost 10-20 times the initial purchase price! (Courtesy Josephine O'Brien)

Small-wheeled pedal machines – a better way of cycling

The joy of looking at your rebuilt, classic small-wheeled machine. (Courtesy Brian Perkins)

And then there will be new spokes – and what about the hubs? And can you re-spoke the wheels yourself or will you need to pay someone else to do that?

Oh well, you say, I'll *upgrade* the bike. Fine – you'll need new 16-inch or 20-inch wheels, and it would be crazy not to get good quality rims, hubs and spokes – with new tyres, of course. Then there's the new seat, the handlebars, the handgrips … And so it goes on – on an old bike, typically *every single component* needs to be replaced or restored.

I've just finished rebuilding a Series 1 Moulton – to be covered in more detail later in this chapter. I bought the bike minus the rear wheel in fair condition for AUD$70 – and around here, that was a bargain. I made a few mistakes along the way that has cost me a bit, but the final cost of the rebuild was about AUD$1100 – around 16 times the initial purchase price! Yes, that's for a bike that has everything I want on it – 5-speed Sturmey Archer internal hub gears, Shutter Precision front hub dynamo, new good quality wheels and tyres, and with the frame stripped right back and powder-coated. But I also wasn't at all extravagant with the selection of mudguards (fenders), brakes, handlebars, seat and seat-post. Cranks, bottom bracket and pedals were all items I already had, and

so cost me nothing. And even if it had all been done on the cheap, to get it looking good and riding well would still have cost a lot.

To restore or rebuild a bike, you'll also need a place where you can work on the machine. That can be done in the middle of the lounge room, but in most domestic situations, it's more likely to be in a shed or workroom. I am lucky to have a well-equipped home workshop – and when rebuilding the Moulton, I used power tools including an angle grinder and electric drill, a bead-blasting cabinet, oxy-acetylene and MIG welding gear, and many hand tools.

So, have I put you off yet?! I hope not, but you do need to be realistic!

And the positives of rebuilding or restoring an older small-wheeled machine? They're great!

First, you will smile whenever you ride your machine, or sit back sipping coffee and looking at it, propped against a wall. If looked after well, a fully-restored machine will last you for decades – and that's a major point to keep in mind when you are justifying the restoration cost.

Second, if you choose to rebuild the bike – rather

This is a '5-metre' (15ft) restoration – it looks fine at that distance. Up close, you can see that fasteners have been painted over, and wheels and brake calipers have rust spots. (Courtesy Brian Walsh)

One advantage when restoring a small-wheeled bike is that very often, the bike used good quality materials and was well made by craftspeople. (Courtesy Bike Friday)

than just restore it – you can make changes that retain the original heritage, but use new, better parts. That's what I did with the Moulton, keeping the marvellous suspension and frame, but replacing everything else. When you do this, you can also develop a machine that better suits your requirements. In terms of gearing, seat, handlebars, pedals, cranks, lights, carriers – they're all choices that you can make for yourself.

Preparing the ground

Before beginning a rebuild or restoration, thoroughly investigate the available support for the bike. Is the manufacturer still in existence, and can they still supply parts? Are there enthusiasts' clubs that have reproduced parts that are not otherwise obtainable, or that have stocks of rarer secondhand parts? Remember, all these machines will have some parts that were especially produced just for these bikes. Local support is best, but online support means that the parts can probably come from anywhere in the world. Are there online support forums where you can ask for advice? Enthusiasts' groups are normally welcoming of people new to the scene and can give great advice and support.

If you are doing a restoration, are all the parts of the bike there? If even an apparently insignificant part is missing, and it proves hard to get, that can stall an entire project. To overcome this issue, can you buy more than one of the bikes? It may initially seem extravagant, but because the initial purchase price is likely to be only a small proportion of the final bill, taking this approach can save you money longer term.

Do you have a friendly local bike shop where you can get help? Even if they don't know much about the specific type of bike you are working on, they'll be able to help in advising on what modern bike parts will fit (if you are taking that route).

First steps

Before you start, take photos of absolutely everything. What looks 'obvious' when the bike is together can look utterly mystifying when the bike is in many small pieces! Does this washer go *here* or *there*? Which was the back end of the mudguard (fender) and which was the front? Where did that gear selector go again?

Then carefully disassemble the bike, taking care

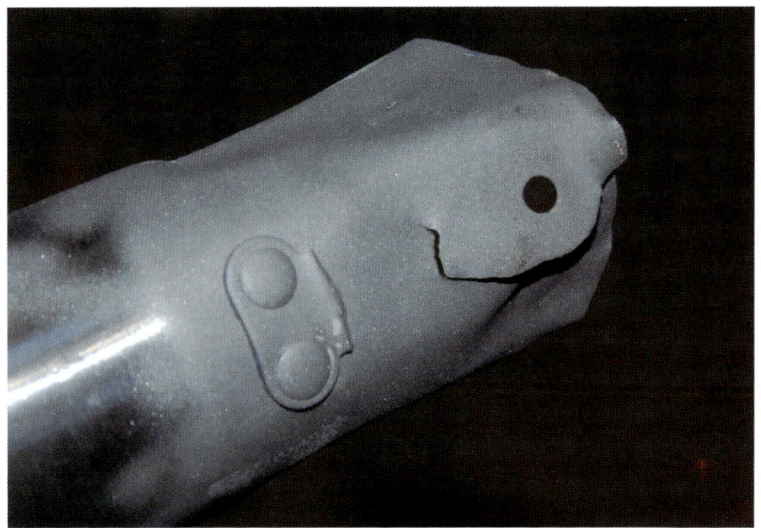

This Moulton mudguard (fender) has a long crack and a broken bracket. The steel is paper-thin, making it very hard to repair in a way that will be durable. This is an example of where having lots of spare parts (eg through buying multiple bikes) is a good approach – just select another mudguard that doesn't need such major repair.

Best results come from stripping back the frame to bare metal, making any required changes, and then painting or powder-coating. (Courtesy Brian Perkins)

As you use the wire brush, you'll often unearth multiple coats of paint that have been applied to the frame over the years – an interesting story in itself. However, in some spots, the frame may be hard to access with the angle grinder and brush. In these locations, you can use a hand-held wire brush. If the paint is still hard to get off, use paint stripper or, if you have access to such a tool, a bead blaster. Be careful not to damage any bearing surfaces or threads.

With the frame and forks stripped, make a close inspection. Hopefully, you will not find any major areas of rust (some surface pitting is OK) but if you do, this will need to be repaired, typically by brazing. Also carefully check the alignment of the frame and forks – any twist or bends can be much more easily corrected when the frame and forks are bare, as adjustment avoids cracking the paint.

With a bare frame, additions can be easily made. For example, braze-on fittings can be purchased for bidons, cable mounts (eg for hub gears) and brakes, and fittings can be installed for lights and a pump. (For small braze-on parts, I recommend Framebuilder Supply of Portland, Oregon, which has a worldwide mail order service). If you don't have brazing facilities, many car and mechanical workshops have oxy-acetylene gear that can do this brazing cheaply and easily. However, before taking the frame to them, ensure the parts are scrupulously clean of paint or grease, and that any locating holes (etc) have already been drilled.

to put every single component into secure storage. For example, for small parts like fasteners and ball bearings, use labelled zip-lock plastic bags. If you are restoring the bike, every part will need to be kept, and if you are rebuilding the bike with many new components, the old parts can be used as samples when sizing or configuring the new parts. Never discard anything until the replacements have been obtained.

The frame

By far the best results will come if the frame is fully stripped of paint – that is, it is taken back to bare metal. An angle grinder spinning a wire brush does this well, but ensure that you wear full eye and hearing protection. Because these wire brushes can shed wires at high speed, any spectators should also be protected.

Upgrades

The most common upgrades are of the wheels, seat and handlebars. By using adapters (eg for the handlebar stem or seat mount), or some tweaking of the front or rear forks (eg by spreading them or closing them a bit), many modern parts can be fitted, even to quite an old bike. However, the combinations and permutations of parts and bikes are endless, so check carefully before spending any money. Try to find out what others have done: many bikes before yours are likely to have been modified or upgraded.

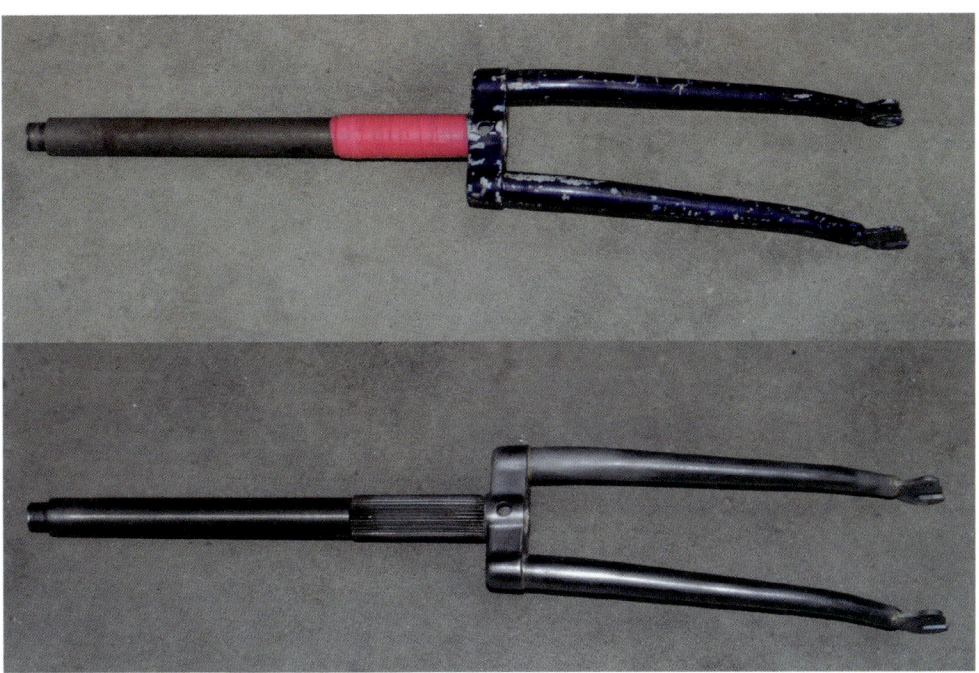

Moulton front forks, before and after wire brushing and bead blasting (the latter for just the hard to get to parts). Note how the splines were protected by multiple layers of tape before cleaning up.

The Moulton

The Series 1 Moulton that I rebuilt makes a good case study. I found the bike at the shop at the local rubbish tip. Usually, the bikes on sale there are run-of-the-mill supermarket models, but I always look in case there is something special. And in this case, there was.

The Moulton was in relatively good condition for something over 50 years old: the frame wasn't dented and the bike was intact, besides missing its rear wheel. However, the chrome front rim was rusty, as were the handlebars, brake levers and calipers. In fact, everything looked tired and unmaintained – it was a bike that had been run into the ground, then put in a dusty shed for 20 years before being dumped.

Before buying it, I made sure that the front and rear suspension systems had movement (ie they weren't

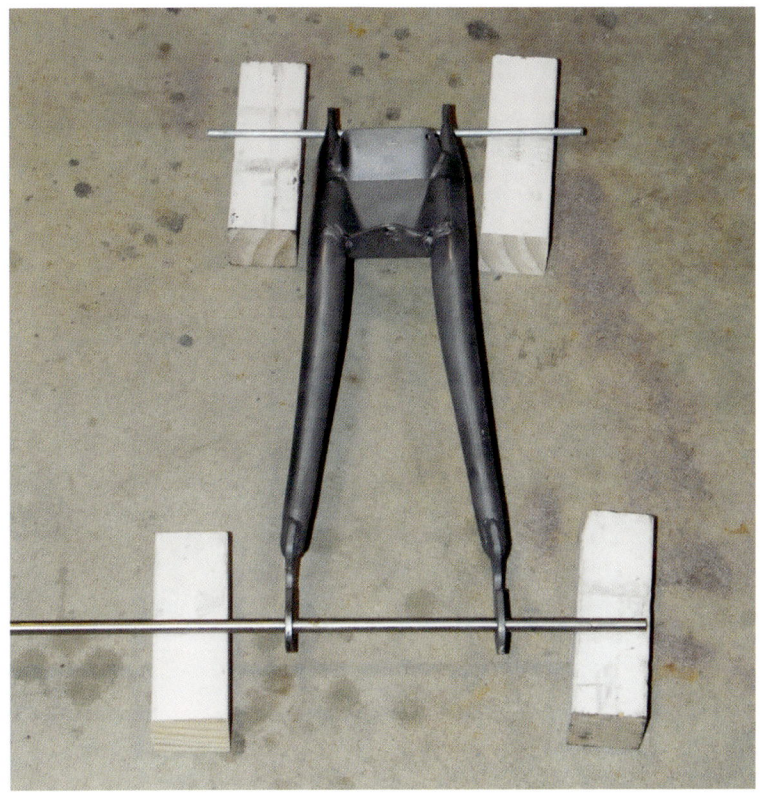

Measuring the amount of twist in the rear suspension forks of the Moulton. Steel rods have been placed through the wheel drop-outs and the suspension pivot holes. Four equal height blocks have been placed on a flat concrete floor. If the forks are untwisted, the rods will rest evenly on all four blocks. In this case, the top-right rod is about 10mm (a little under ½in) above the block. By holding the forks in a vice and using a long lever, they were easily untwisted.

frozen solid) – an important step with any suspension bike.

Initial disassembly was straightforward. Because I knew that I'd be doing a major upgrade rather than restoration (with a wheel missing, I couldn't restore it easily, and I was surprised by how heavy everything was as it came off the frame – better to go lighter and newer, anyway), frozen nuts and bolts were cut off as required. I put aside the front forks assembly (this incorporates the suspension) and then stripped the frame of paint, using a combination of wire brushing and bead-blasting.

Under the three layers of paint, the frame was in near-perfect condition, with only the tiniest pitting in a few areas from rust. (This pitting was so slight that by the time the frame was undercoated and then powder-coated, it wasn't visible.)

Chuffed with how things were going, I then made my first major mistake. Looking at the front suspension fork assembly, I just couldn't see how it came apart. I then browsed the web, finding a number of sites devoted to just this topic. Apparently, I read, there was a screw buried deep inside the forks that had to be undone, then a collar unscrewed – and then it all just came apart. But I couldn't see any screw! I read further on-line and then found a description of how one person had drilled out the screw, working from the other end of the forks and using a drill-bit silver-soldered to a long rod to give the required extension.

But little did I know, this person's website instructions were all wrong!

In happy ignorance, I followed these instructions – only to completely wreck the front suspension system. Yes, you can get the suspension apart in this way – but you then need to make new parts to replace those destroyed, and a whole bunch of other issues are created.

To say I was crestfallen was an understatement – I was devastated. Oddly, I also felt that I'd done the wrong thing by the bike – here I'd promised it a new life, and in the first few hours I'd already broken it.

However, all was not lost. The Moulton Preservation section of the Moulton Club in the UK can supply new (secondhand) front forks and suspension, complete with new (reproduction) plastic bushes on which the suspension slides. It cost a lot to freight these parts to the other side of the world, but at least I had a working suspension again.

My next step was to fit a new bottom bracket bearing, chain wheels, cranks and pedals. I used parts left over from my recumbent trike building. The new bottom bracket bearing screwed straight into the Moulton frame, although, as it was a bit wider, I needed to make up two spacers. (I am sure a direct replacement could have been obtained, but since I already had these parts, it made sense to use them.)

Wheels were the next step. The Moulton runs 16-inch wheels, and the most common high quality small-wheeled bike with this size of wheel is the Brompton. Therefore, when sourcing the new wheels, I scoured the web for Brompton wheels. Best prices and availability seem to come from Taiwanese suppliers (Taiwan has an enormous cycling industry). I chose a 5-speed dynamo wheelset comprising Alex DA16, (16 x 1⅜in, 349mm), 28-hole rims with DT Swiss Champion 14-gauge spokes, and DT Swiss brass nipples. The rear wheel was equipped with a Sturmey Archer S-RF5(W) 5-speed hub, and the front with a

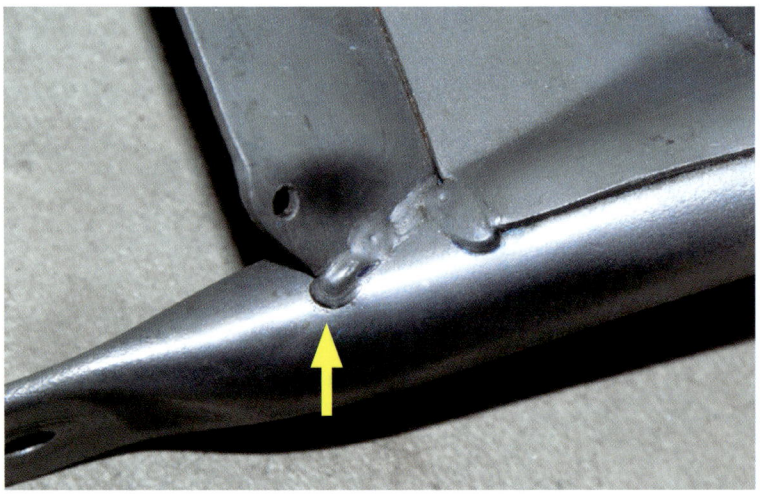

Moulton rear forks are known for cracking, and on this example, one of the welds had just started pulling out of the tube (arrow). Stripping back to bare metal allows you to find faults like this that can then be repaired.

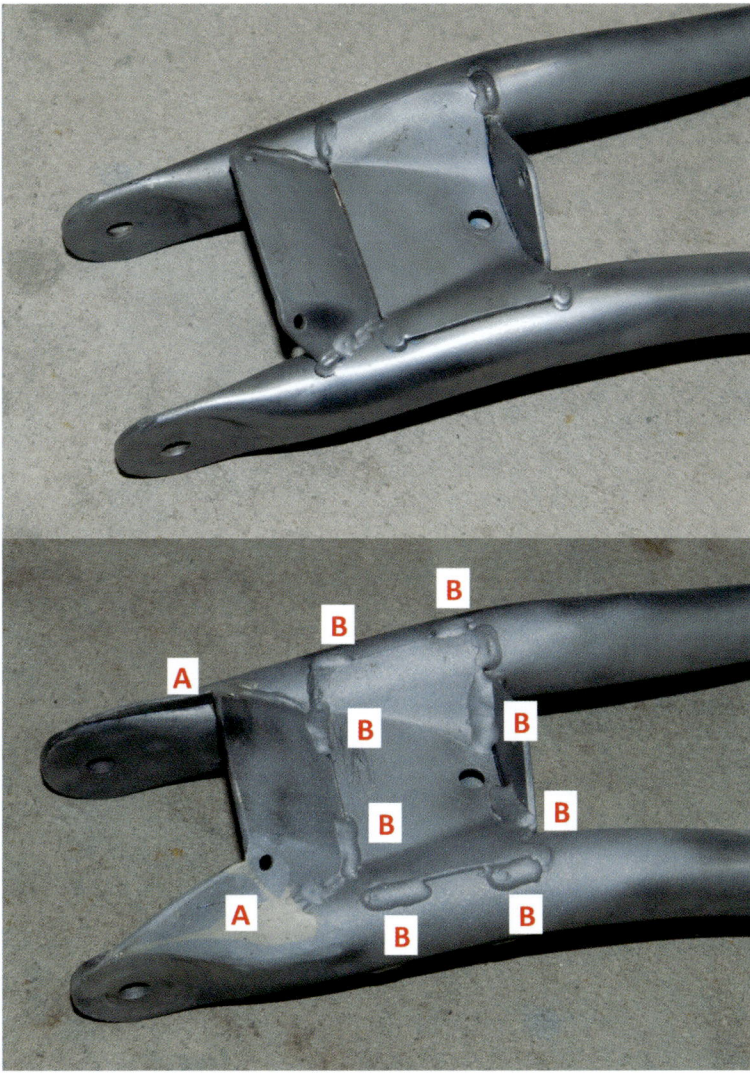

The rear Moulton forks, before and after strengthening. The triangular gussets were nickel-bronze brazed into place (A), and extra MIG welds were added to the crossmember (B).

While I was waiting for the wheels to arrive, I inspected the rear forks. These are made in an unusual way for bicycle items, being MIG welded as well as brazed. Series 1 Moulton rear forks are also known for cracking at a specific location, one that is placed under great tension when the rear suspension compresses (and shears) its rubber suspension block. And, when I looked closely through a magnifying glass, I could see that while there was no major cracking, a weld was just starting to pull out of the tube. Before I repaired this, I also inspected the rear forks for twist. Again, these Series 1 forks are renowned for twisting. And again, yes – the forks on my bike were twisted by about 10mm (just under ½in).

So the first step was to remove the twist (easily done by placing the forks in a vice and then using a long lever through the fork legs to untwist them) and the second step was to braze strengthening gussets into place to prevent further cracking. I used nickel-bronze brazing to do this (nickel bronze is very strong) but it could also have been done by MIG welding – a common process that all mechanical workshops can do for you. I also added some extra MIG welds to the box-like member at the base of the forks assembly – this gives the forks more torsional strength and so should stop twisting in the future.

After adding a new seat and seat post (the latter needing a shim made from an aluminium drink can – a standard 25.4mm (1in) post being fractionally smaller than the Moulton tube) the bike could be test-ridden for the first time. But why would anyone ride a bike with a bare unpainted frame, no brakes yet and the old corroded handlebars put back on? The answer to that is in multiple parts.

First, I'd never ridden a Moulton before – and I couldn't wait to find out what it was like! Second, there was lots I wanted to find out before proceeding any further. Things like: what handlebar height and reach would suit me? What overall gearing did I want? Should I add brass braze-on mounts for a bidon (or two), and where would they best fit without causing leg obstruction? If I'd had a spare, fully working Moulton Series 1 at hand, these questions could have

Shutter Precision SV-9 hub dynamo. Add Schwalbe Marathon Plus tyre and tubes – and there went nearly half of the budget!

Note: Brompton front forks are narrower than the Moulton forks, so the Moulton forks needed to be closed up a little to work with the Brompton-sized wheels. This was easily done by using a bench vice to push the forks closer together, with the metalwork protected from the vice jaws by scrap wood. The rear forks are a similar width to the Brompton.

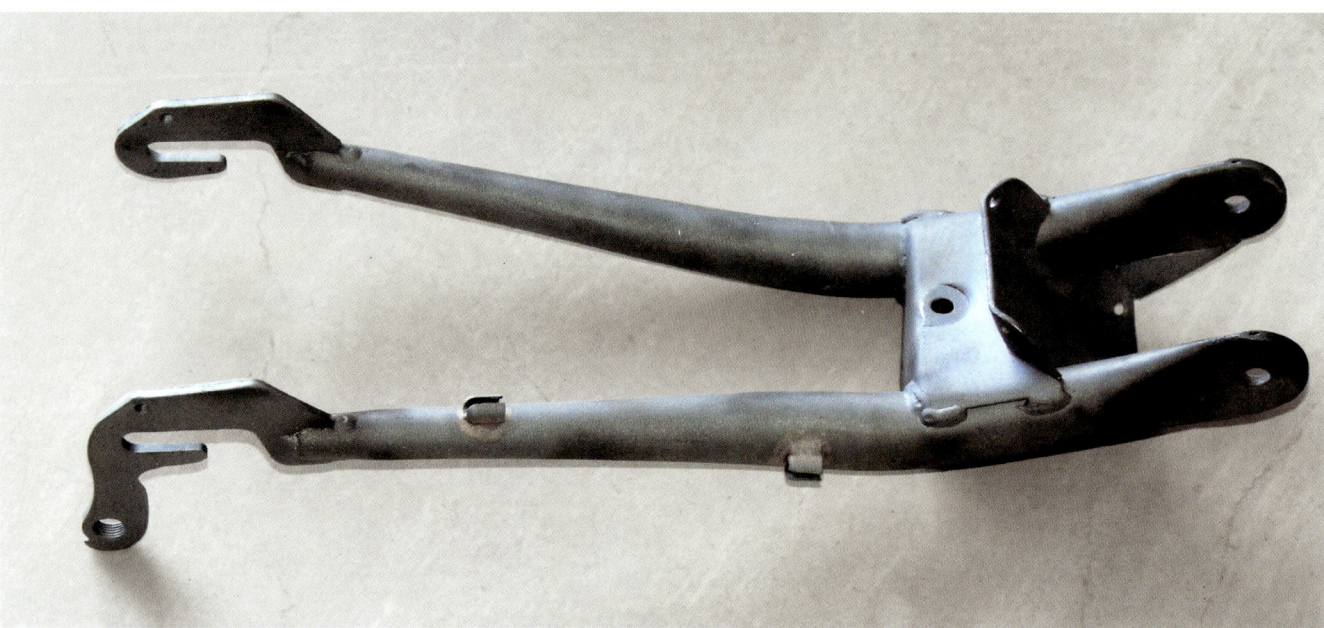

The rebuilt rear forks, complete with added derailleur mount and brazed-on cable end-mounts.

The carriers

I chose to make new front and rear carriers for the Moulton. The original rear carrier was a bit battered, and while I straightened it, I could never get it perfect. Also, I wanted to be able to carry rear panniers, but the original carrier didn't have the downwards support needed to do this (and, due to the presence of the rear suspension, there's no other frame support available). No front carrier was supplied with the bike.

The rear carrier was modelled along the original's lines, but was wider and longer. It was made from high tensile, thin-walled steel tube, 12mm (½in) in diameter. I got the tube from the same place as the bike – the shop at the local rubbish tip. The tube came in the form of a child's safety gate equipped with vertical bars. Before buying, I tested that the tube was good quality by squeezing some of the bars together and seeing if the tubing sprang back into shape. Tubing that springs back into position is suitable for use; in contrast, tubing that takes a permanent 'set' (bend) is not.

The front carrier uses the original Moulton carrier mounts, but, like the rear carrier, is a little larger and stronger than the original.

Of course, building carriers like these needs a lot more facilities than those required for just a simple bike restoration, with tube bending (I used a low-cost hand bender) and brazing facilities required.

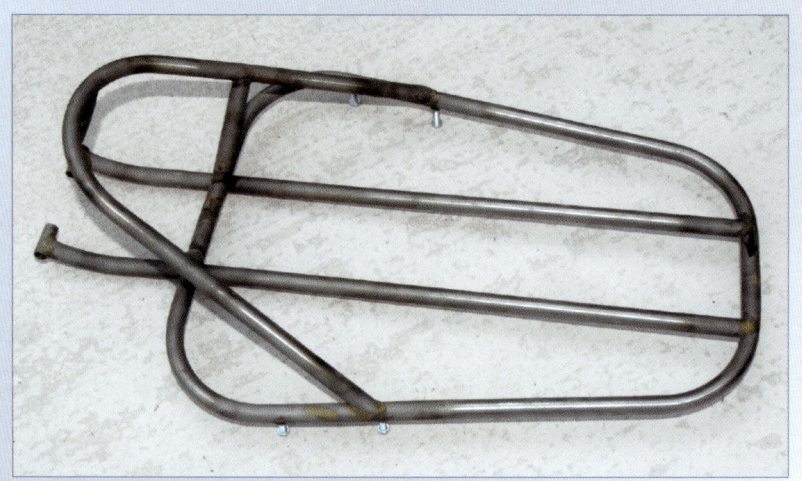

The newly-made front carrier, prior to powder-coating. The tubing was bent using a small hand-bender before being brazed together.

all been answered – but I didn't, thus explaining the test ride of the incomplete bike.

Riding just around my yard showed two things – the suspension was working very well … and I needed brakes! The brakes are in fact a good example of feeling your way. Measurements showed the required reach needed for the new calipers, but what measurements couldn't show me was if they'd fit –

especially on the back where clearances are tight. Neither did an intensive web search help – people had fitted new brakes to Series 1 Moultons, but how they'd done so wasn't clear. If I had a local bike shop, some of these questions may have been able to be answered by an expert, but without such a facility, in the end I simply took a punt and ordered some new brakes.

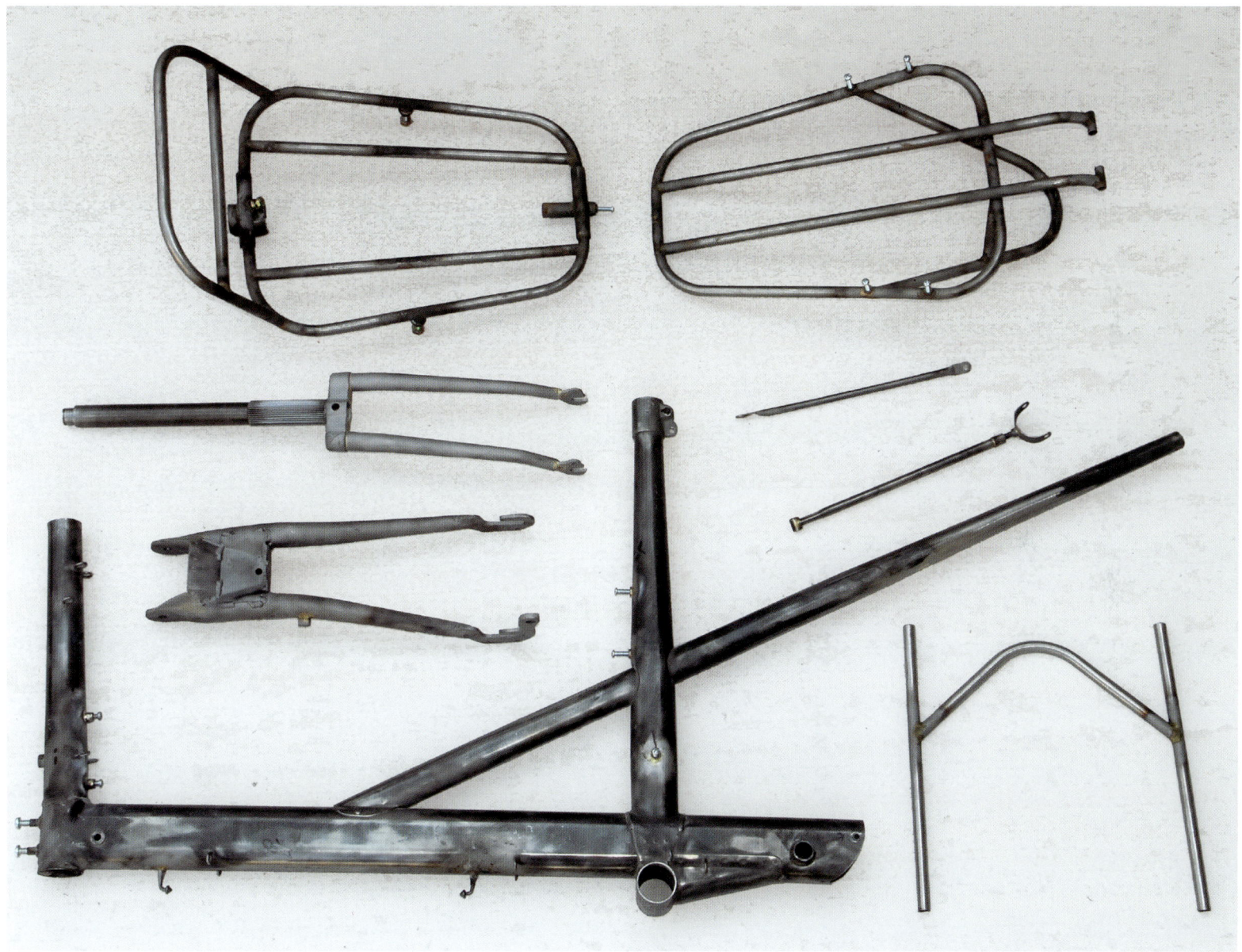

The parts prior to powder-coating. From the top: the newly-constructed carriers, the front and rear forks, the rear carrier support pieces, and the main frame. Lower-right is the extension that attaches to the bottom of the rear carrier and supports panniers.

Small-wheeled pedal machines – a better way of cycling

Those I bought were Tektro R559, that had the required long reach, and came with external nuts rather than the more modern recessed (ie larger diameter) nuts. The front caliper fitted fine, but the rear fouled the rubber suspension block. However, if the clearance between the brake block and rim was dropped to a minimum, some judicious belt sanding of the caliper arm could be used to give the required clearance. I write this not to tell you how to fit brake calipers to a Moulton Series 1, but to show how it's very likely that

Lighting system

I chose to use a self-developed lighting system on the Moulton. If you're interested in electronics and want to use a hub dynamo, it's a fairly easy system to replicate.

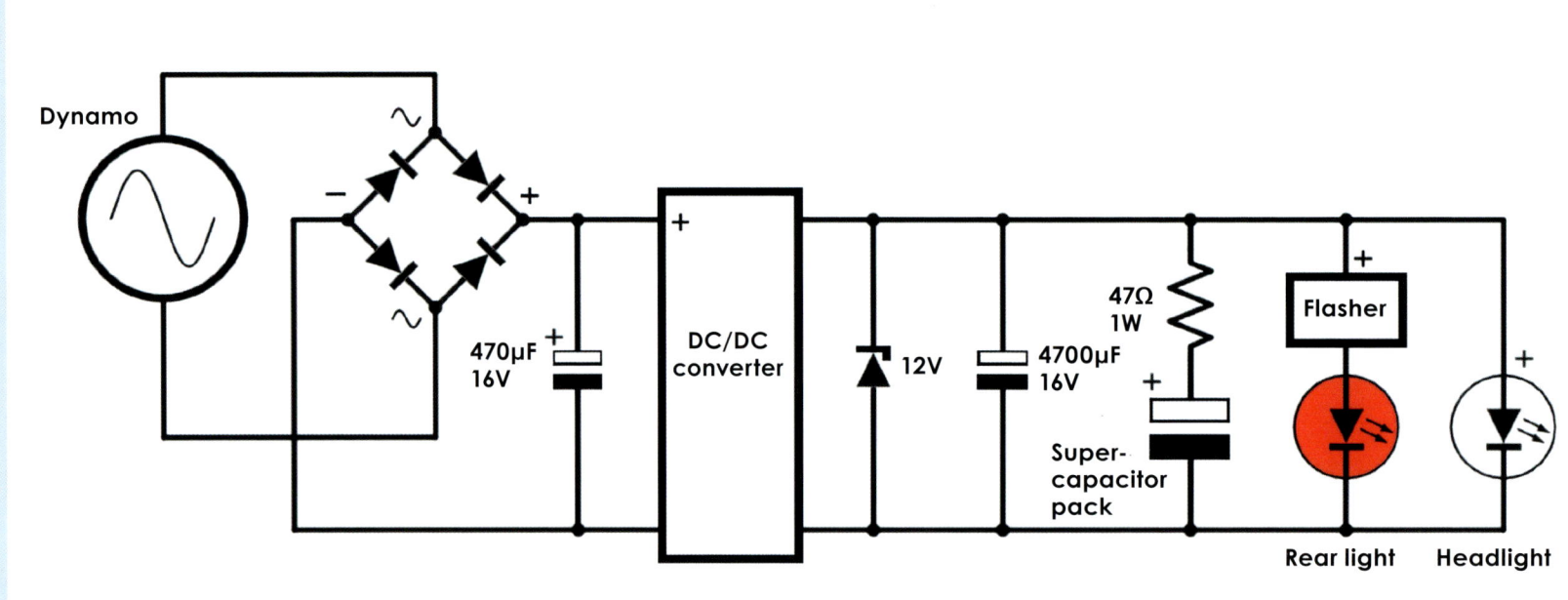

A Shutter Precision SV-9 hub dynamo is the basis of the system. The dynamo's output is rectified and smoothed, and then fed to a DC/DC buck/boost converter, set to 12V. On the output of the converter, a 12V Zener diode clips the spike that otherwise occurs when the converter first starts to operate. The 4700µF capacitor reduces headlight flicker caused by the alternating load of the rear flasher. A supercapacitor pack feeds through a 47Ω resistor that limits the capacitor pack's charge rate, and so doesn't overly impact the brightness of the lights. The rear light is fed through a flasher module, and the headlight is powered directly from the 12V feed – both front and rear LEDs are designed for 12V use. The system gives bright lights from a walking pace, and keeps the lights running for a period when the bike has stopped moving.

some tweaking and/or careful parts selection will be needed when upgrading an old small-wheeled bike.

On the other hand, the new stem and handlebars were bought and fitted without any issues at all. I'd been riding with the old 'lady's style' handlebars – and I really liked them! However, they were heavy and I'd prefer that the handgrips not point towards the rider (so making pulling on them hard) but instead be transverse in angle. A replacement alloy stem that fits within the standard suspension tube recess was easily

The LED headlight was made from a 64mm convex glass lens, a shortened aluminium drinking cup and a LED light. The plastic rim is a cut-down plumbing cap. The light gives a broad, even beam and has a power of only 0.8W.

This buck/boost module maintains a constant output voltage. This allows a constant system voltage, even when working with the variable-speed bicycle dynamo. The AC from the dynamo is rectified and filtered before being fed to this module.

The tail-light uses a 12V red LED assembly and flasher module. Average power is just 0.25W yet it is visible from over 100 metres/yards.

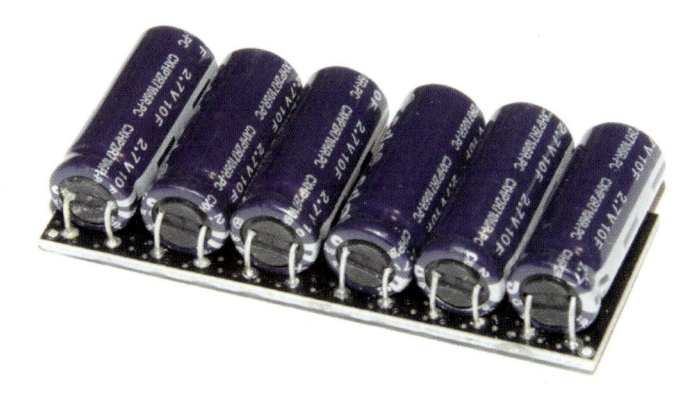

This supercapacitor pack is used to maintain light output, even when the bike is stationary.

(Continues on next page)

The completed electronics. The rectifier and filter capacitor are at left. The top board is the DC/DC converter, with the supercapacitor board beneath. At the right, just visible, is the Zener diode that clips any excessive output before the DC/DC converter starts to function, and the capacitor that smooths light flicker before the supercapacitor pack is charged.

The assembly (just!) slides into a short length of 44mm (1¾in) diameter plastic pipe, and is sealed at each end by caps. Visible here is the flasher module, as supplied with the flashing LED used for the tail-light. I chose to subsequently pot the electronics in epoxy to make them vibration- and water-proof.

The module containing the electronics can be seen here. The lights work whenever the bicycle is being ridden – there is no on/off switch.

New frame components brazed into place and ready for powder-coating. One of two pump mounts is shown (left), and two bidon mounts (right), complete with inserted screws to protect the threads from the powder-coat.

sourced, and replacement alloy handlebars weren't far behind. The cost was low, fitting easy and they give me my desired riding position – in fact, riding *positions,* as the handlebars I chose have both high and low handgrips.

Frame finishing

With the Moulton frame finished (complete with its added-on brazed fittings), it was time to look at frame finishing. With the frame back to bare metal, either painting or powder-coating could be done.

Painting is most common, and is much cheaper than powder-coating. If painting a bare frame, ensure that it is scrupulously clean of grease – wipe it over with a lint-free cloth wet with paint thinners, and then let it dry. You can then take the traditional primer/undercoat/top-coat approaches, or instead use a high-quality paint designed to go on over bare metal. I must say that I've had more success with the latter approach, and I recommend Rust-Oleum Ultra Cover 2X spray paint. If in doubt, test your proposed paint approach on some scrap steel prepared in the same way as the bicycle frame. Good results should

not only look attractive but be resistant to chipping.

However, instead of painting, I chose to use powder-coating. In this process the frame is first blasted and then primed with a suitable paint. A fine coloured powder is then electrostatically applied to the frame, and then the frame is placed in an oven. The powder melts to form a glossy, very hard-wearing coating. Powder-coating is widely used in industry and requires specialised application facilities. Expect to pay 4-5 times the price of painting. Ensure you give clear instructions to the powder-coater about areas that should *not* be coated (eg bottom-bracket threads) and place sacrificial screws in all tapped holes (eg mounts for drink holders). These screws prevent the powder-coating from clogging the threads; after the powder-coating has been done, the screws can be undone and thrown away. Incidentally, the bare frame *must* be primed or undercoated before being powder-coated, otherwise in humid climates the metalwork can rust under the powder-coating.

The range of colours available from powder-coaters is not as wide as for paint, but there are still

The Moulton being ridden part-way through the rebuild. Doing this allows you to check that everything is working prior to committing to the final version of the bike. For example, here, I was yet to install any of the braze-on fittings, and was ensuring that the lighting system (just taped into place) was effective. I also chose to use different handlebars on the final bike.

plenty to choose from. I decided with the Moulton to go for an orange main frame – and black everything else.

The completed bike

I am very happy with the completed Moulton. As you'd expect, considering that I modified it with just me as the rider in mind, the gearing is perfect, the riding position good, and the lighting system works really well. But – and here's the key point for this book – I also love the Moulton's agility, the way the suspension copes so very well with poor road surfaces, and the surprising stiffness of the frame. It honestly puts a smile on my face every time I ride it.

The completed Moulton. Just the orange frame and the front and rear forks remain standard – along with the superb suspension, of course.

The carrier is modelled along original lines, but is wider and taller. It was formed from tubing using a hand bender, with the tubes brazed together.

A bag mounting block from a Brompton has been added. When required, this can be removed and a front carrier fitted. Also visible here is the very compact Shutter Precision SV-9 hub dynamo.

A complete buyer's guide to electric bicycles, including the types of bike available, what to look for, and why you should buy one. Packed with useful contacts, including importers, websites and magazines, advice on where you can ride, and the law. Also includes battery charging and maintenance info, as well as basic cycle maintenance.

ISBN: 978-1-845849-39-9

Paperback • 19.5x13.9cm • 64 pages • 101 colour pictures

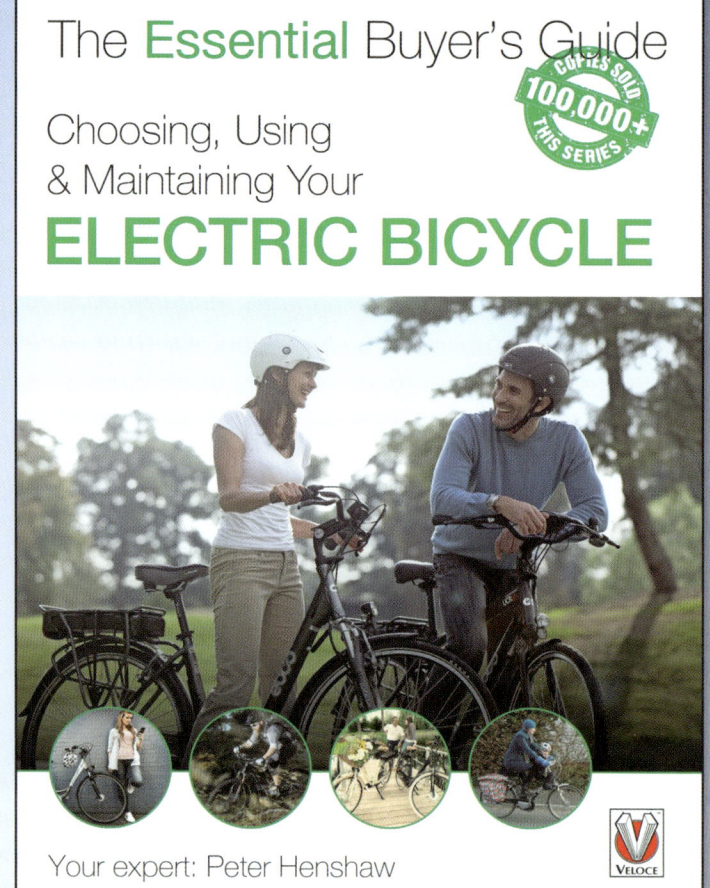

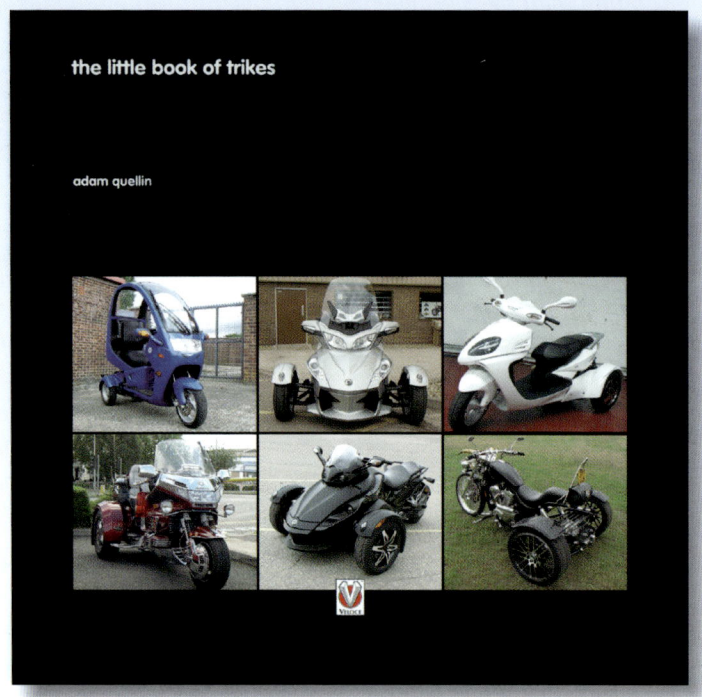

A celebration of the many motor trikes and three-wheeled motorcycles produced since the early days of motoring. Taking us right up to the present day, this book covers a wide range of machines from mild to wild, accompanied by original colour photographs. Featuring easy-to-read captions with minimum jargon: it will delight both enthusiasts and the novices alike.

ISBN: 978-1-845842-95-6

Paperback • 14x14cm • 96 pages • 76 colour pictures

For more information and price details, see www.veloce.co.uk

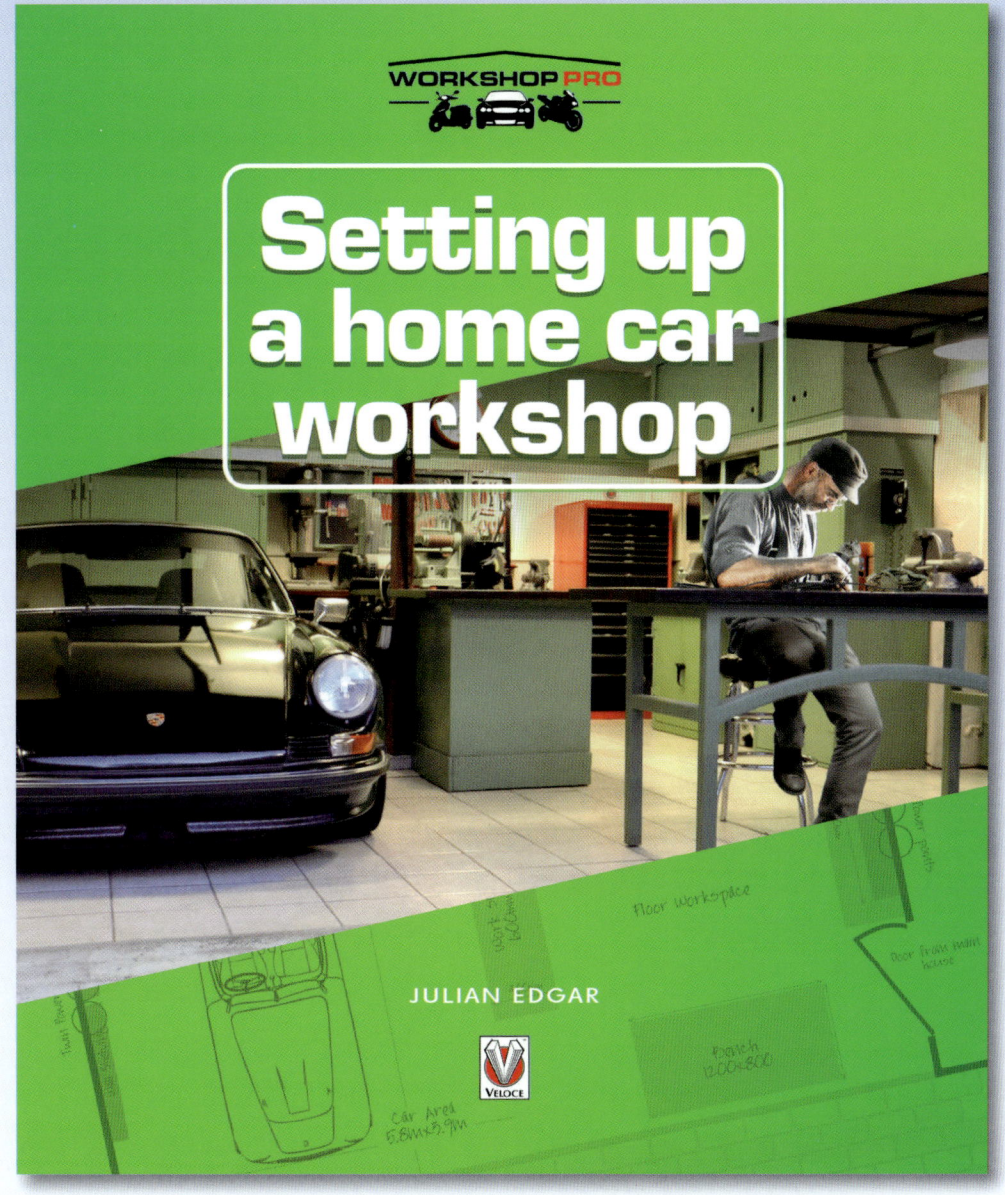

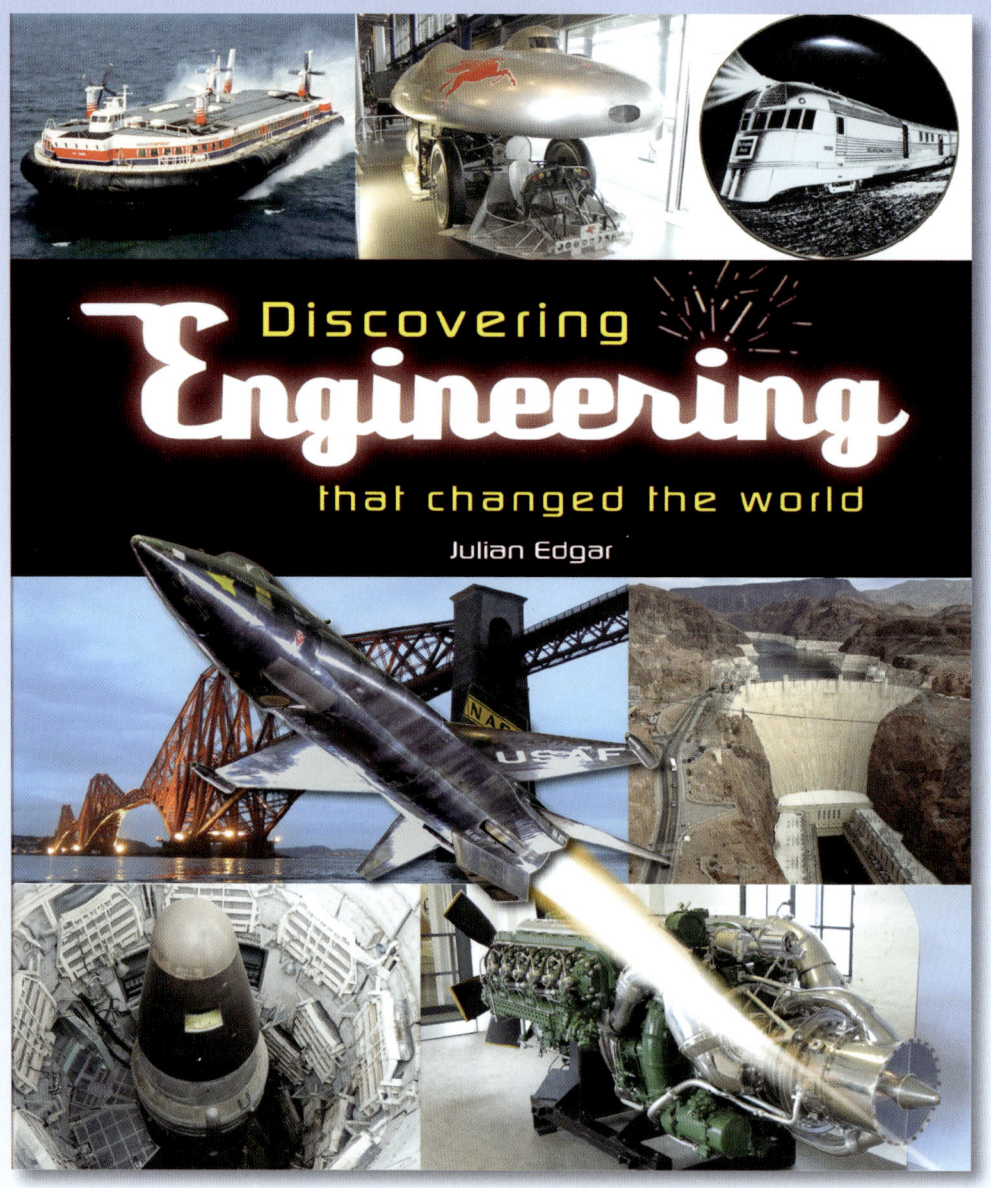

In this unique book, author Julian Edgar takes you around the world to see an astonishing series of engineering marvels. Through over 170 original photos, accompanied by a thoroughly researched text, you'll experience the first rocket range, the fastest cars, and the awesome technology of the Cold War.

• ISBN: 978-1-787113-55-8

Paperback • 25x20.7cm• 144 pages • 174 pictures

For more about this fascinating book see Julian Edgar's videos on YouTube: https://youtu.be/rZHFQuWGUd0

For more information and price details, see www.veloce.co.uk
• email: info@veloce.co.uk • Tel: +44(0)1305 260068

Index

Advantages
  folding bikes 31-34
  recumbent trikes 44-47
  small-wheeled bikes 7-9

Bickerton 28
Bike Friday 8, 15, 32, 36, 77
Birdy 39, 67-74
Brompton 9, 14, 18, 20, 31, 33, 35, 40, 51, 52,
  59-64, 66
Burley trailers 60-64, 66

Cadence 13-16
Carrier construction 82
Carrying goods 7
Clothing 19
Commuting 51-56
  equipment 54
  planning 52
  tools 55

Dahon 34, 37
Damping – suspension 11-12
Design 7-20, 22-26
Development – metres of 13
Disadvantages
  folding bikes 34-35

recumbent trikes 43-44
small-wheeled bikes 9-10

Fixed-frame bikes 21-30
  commuting 52
Folding bikes 31-41
  commuting 52
  packing 33
  selection 37-39
Frame
  finishing 87
  restoration 78

Gear – metres of development 13
Gearing 13-17
  folding bikes 36
  range 17
  touring 18
Greenspeed 42-50

Hub dynamo 19-20, 84-86

Lighting 19, 55, 84-86

Moulton 6, 11, 16, 19, 21-27, 55, 58, 75-84

Index

Moulton, Alex 22-27

Natural frequency 12

Raleigh 20 28
Reach – Pacific Cycles 68-74
Recumbent bikes 47
Recumbent trikes 42-50
   advantages 44-47
   commuting 53
   disadvantages 43-44
   folding 50
   selection 47
Restoration and rebuilding 75-90

Speed 7
Springing (suspensions) 10-12
Static deflection 12

Suspension 10, 24-25, 79-82
   folding bikes 35
   trikes 47-48

Touring 57-74
   bike transport 57
   children 60, 61, 62, 63
   equipment 59, 64-66
   Kangaroo Island 66-74
   self-supported 58
   trailer 60, 61
Trikes (see recumbent trikes)

Velotechnik Scorpion fs 48
Visibility – clothing 19

Wheel size 7-10, 47
Workplaces – bicycle friendly 54